(새번역)

THE PEOPLE OF PILGRIM'S PROGRESS

SHI-RYONG PARK

Ark House Press
arkhousepress.com

© 2025 Shi-Ryong PARK

All rights reserved. Apart from any fair dealing for the purpose of study, research, criticism, or review, as permitted under the Copyright Act, no part may be reproduced by any process without written permission.

Cataloguing in Publication Data:
Title: The People of Pilgram's Progress
ISBN: 978-1-7641051-6-3 (pbk)
Subjects: [FIC042090] FICTION / Christian / Biblical; [FIC042100] FICTION / Christian / Contemporary; [REL012040] RELIGION / Christian Living / Inspirational;

Illustrations by Shi-Ryong Park
Design by initiateagency.com

Table of Contents

Table of Contents iii

Introduction v

Chapter 1: What should I do? 1

Chapter 2: Worldly Wiseman 12

Chapter 3: The Wicket Gate 24

Chapter 4: The Interpreter's House 34

Chapter 5: Simple·Slothful·Presumption. 43

Chapter 6: The Hill Difficulty 52

Chapter 7: A Beautiful House 62

Chapter 8: Avoluon 73

Chapter 9: The Valley of Shadows 86

Chapter 10: The Marketplace of Vanities. 96

Chapter 11: Mr. Gripe-man 106

Chapter 12: The Prison of Despair 117

Chapter 13: The Delectable Mountain 124

Chapter 14: A Little Faith 134

Chapter 15: Atheist and Ignorance 145

Chapter 16: The Land of Beulah 155

Chapter 17: The River of Death 167

Bibliography 178

Illustrations 180

About the Author 196

Endorsements 197

INTRODUCTION

The first time I read John Bunyan's The Book of Pilgrim's Progress was in high school, when it was a highly recommended classic in our World Literature class. By the time I picked it up again, I was at an age when I couldn't read without using a magnifying glass. I went to church and believed in Jesus, but I still had a fear of death.

As I watched "Christian" cross the river of death with Hopeful, I realised that "death is not the end of our life, but the beginning of a new life." As I lived through the panoramic passage of seventy years, I realised that Christian was me.

As a Christian, my journey to study in Germany to become a biologist, and the "Beautiful Home" where the Christian of the Pilgrim's Progress stopped for a while, was my pilgrimage. As a biologist, I worked on the stork reintroduction project and praised the merciful God who created all that is good and true. Unable to compete with the frenzy of digital games and the pet industry, the market of vanity that has taken over the cinema, YouTube and the internet, I had to close the stork reintroduction project and I was devastated. But as I followed the Christian pilgrimage, I was reborn as a person with heavenly hopes.

THE PEOPLE OF PILGRIM'S PROGRESS

The Bible records that a woman with haemophilia touched the hem of Jesus' garment and was instantly healed (Mark 5:28-34). Jesus said, "Your faith has saved you" (v.34), and it happened once and for all. My hope and prayer is that as I watercolour the characters in the book, I too will touch the hem of Jesus' garment.

As I read the book, I thought about the characters in it - Obstinate, Pliable, Sloth, Presumption, Formalist, Hypocrisy, Ignorance, Talkative, Mr. Save-all, Little faith, Truth, and Hopeful. While staying at the Pilgrim House in Gapyeong, the only one of its kind in the world, I was inspired by the figures of the sculptures on the pilgrimage route to Pilgrim's Progress and began to paint them.

I first learned about watercolor on Hanji-paper when I studied abroad in Germany, where I was introduced to the work of expressionist artist and watercolor master Emil Nolde (German 1867-1956). The works in this book are the result of my becoming Nolde's artificial intelligence (AI) after studying over 6,000 of his works. Of course, there are differences. The difference is that an AI cannot have faith, but I have faith that the Lord is in me, with the assurance of salvation by touching the hem of His garment.

The first thing I saw when I was born was my father, mother, and family. As I grew up, I saw friends and relatives, neighbors and animals; I can't count on my fingers the number of people I've met in my life. One person who dramatically changed my life as a young adult was John Bunyan, the author of *The Pilgrim's Progress*.

He was born in 1628 in a small village called Elstow near Bedford, England, the son of a poor tinker. He learned the tinker's trade from his father and married a woman who came to him with only two books. He first came to know Jesus through reading his wife's two prized possessions, and was so moved by the Reverend John Gifford that he was baptised in 1653. He then began to witness to the gospel with irresistible zeal. Even when Charles II suppressed all religions except the Church of England in 1660, he continued to preach, and was arrested and imprisoned for three months. When he disobeyed orders not to preach again, he was arrested again and imprisoned for 12 years until 1672. It was during this time that Bunyan wrote *The Pilgrim's Progress*.

As a professing Christian, I'm going to look at the characters in The Rise and Fall of the Stork, and I'm going to do it with a stork that has been my companion for half my life. I love my stork and my neighbours, and they have loved me and my stork very much, even though they have sometimes led me into the valley of the shadow of death.

I am now in the twilight of my life. The river of death that Christians must cross is at hand, and I stand at its mouth, climbing Mount Inwang, the nearest to where I live. Every day I watch the mountain pigeons, the crows, the magpies, the wrens, the chickadees, the woodpeckers, the kestrels, the birdcatchers, the cicadas, the ants, as they make their last farewells on this other planet. The end of the conversation is always gratitude to God for sending me to this earth to make love with storks and talk to animals, and for the grace and rebirth I have received in the face of the river of death. My life today is a great gift.

I no longer have to live a dreary life where there always seems to be a dark cloud hanging over me. For the "Spirit of life in Christ" (Romans 8:2) has blown in like a mighty wind and has swept away all the dark clouds in the sky. I sing and shout for joy! And to the glory of God through Jesus the Messiah, I am about to leave my past as a scientist behind and begin a new journey to God.

CHAPTER 1
WHAT SHOULD I DO?

When I first began to believe in Jesus, I saw him only as a teacher of the truths of the world, so I opened my Bible to a passage and thought that he must have had an extraordinary childhood. I remember reading it and thinking of the young Jesus as a child prodigy. But Jesus was not a prodigy, not a teacher of mankind. He was not even what we would call a saint in the conventional sense of the word. He was just a manifestation of God in a body like ours, but he was still the living God. John Bunyan began to write The Pilgrim's Progress in the form of a stranger who feared God's judgement.

Christian, the hero of the story, wandered through the wilderness of the world until he came to a cave where he decided to spend the night and unpacked his things. He fell asleep and dreamt that he saw a man dressed in dirty clothes standing outside his house. He had a book in his hand and a heavy burden on his back. He opened the book and started to read. As he read, he trembled with tears. Later, as if he couldn't stand it any longer, he said aloud, "What should I do?"

What should I do? (2023)

The book the Christians opened was the Bible. What in it made them shudder?

The day of the Lord will come as a thief in the night, in the which the heavens shall pass away with a great noise, and the elements shall be burned with fervent fire, and the principalities of the earth and all that is therein shall be revealed (2 Peter 3:10).

Christian continued reading the Bible. After a while he remembered the heavy burden he was carrying on his back and he began to realise that it was his sins, for it was filled with all the lies he had told, all the times he had deceived others, all the times he had criticised others and spoken curses.

He convinced his wife and children, "If we don't find a way to be saved, we will all die, not just me, but my whole family." His family were very surprised to hear this, not because they believed him, but because they thought he had gone mad. In fact, they treated him as if he were insane. With little persuasion from his family, Christian had no choice but to set off on his pilgrimage alone.

The days of wandering

I've had my moments of despair and frustration. There was a time in high school when I was very lost. Questions like, why was I put on this earth and what happens when I die? Of course, I didn't think I was burdened with sin like Christian in Bunyan's novel. I had three older sisters above me and two younger brothers and a younger sister below me. We didn't have much money.

I'm about to open an old, dusty, 60-year-old diary I've been flicking through for years. We lived in a cul-de-sac with a broken cement staircase, and the houses on either side of the staircase were crowded together.

One day I saw my older sister taking some clothes my mother had saved and going upstairs to meet her boyfriend. I told my mother about it. Although we were poor, my parents were very strict with their daughter. Probably all parents with daughters were like that in those days. After that, my sister was grounded and I had no choice but to keep an eye on her. Then she suddenly went blind. She finally died without waking up during an operation to remove a tumour from the back of her optic nerve. That's when I got a deep sense of what life is all about.

My sister's boyfriend next door (2011)

After that, a friend introduced me to a Bible Baptist church near my high school, pastored by an American missionary. It was there that I first realised I was a sinner and was baptised.

When I first became a believer, instead of accepting the idea that Jesus came to earth to die for our sins, I had so many questions about Jesus. The most intense question I had was this.

"How did Mary, the mother of Jesus, give birth to Jesus alone without sleeping with her husband Joseph?"

This was a natural question for a scientist. I knew that even in animals, females sometimes give birth by themselves through unfertilised ovulation without mating with a male, so while I look at Jesus with faith now, the Bible was full of questions for me then.

Of course I also wondered about Jesus' childhood, but there is only one mention of Jesus' childhood in the Bible. He's having a heated discussion with the rabbis in the temple (Luke 2:41-52). This image made me think, "Wow, the boy Jesus was pretty special," rather than Jesus the Son of God.

The boy Jesus debating with the rabbis in the temple (2021)

The Bible doesn't tell us how Jesus grew up. All it says is that he grew up to be a young man of about 30, was baptised by John the Baptist, fasted for 40 days in the wilderness and overcame the temptations of the devil. He lived a short symbiosis of three years on earth. I'm going to read about his three-year symbiosis in the Bible and make a watercolour painting.

Tempted (2022)

Tempted

Jesus was led by the Holy Spirit into the desert to be tempted (Matthew 4:1-11). There the devil was waiting for him. Jesus prepared for the temptation by fasting for forty days and forty nights, so his hunger was at its peak, and the devil took advantage of this in his first test.

"Since you are the Son of God, speak to these stones and make them become loaves of bread."

Jesus replied by quoting Deuteronomy.

"Man does not live by bread alone. There must be a continuing word from the mouth of God.

For the second test, the devil took Jesus to the holy city, sat him on the pinnacle of the temple and said.

"You are the Son of God, jump down and look."

The devil then quoted Psalm 91 to drive home his point.

"He has given you angels to guard you. They will receive you and keep you from bruising your toe on a stone".

Again Jesus fired back, this time quoting another verse from Deuteronomy.

"Do not tempt the Lord your God.

For the third temptation, the devil took Jesus to the top of a huge mountain. The devil pointed out all the nations of the earth and their great splendour, as if in a show of good will. Then he said.

"It is all yours. All you have to do is fall down and worship me and it's yours".

Jesus cut him off.

"Get behind me, Satan!"

And a third time he drove a wedge by quoting Deuteronomy.

"The Lord your God is the only one you are to worship. Serve him with single-mindedness."

Then the temptation was over and the devil went away. Instead, angels came and ministered to Jesus.

I remember the scene of Jesus being tempted by the devil 2000 years ago.

This scene has been etched in my mind ever since I painted 'Tempted' (2022).

The Lord clearly tells his disciples to 'watch and pray that you may not enter into temptation' (Mark 14:38).

I promise to pray every day at the beginning and end of this pilgrimage.

My youth

The devil stood before Jesus, hungry from 40 days of fasting, and demanded that he worship him with promises of worldly goods and status. Seeing Jesus defeat the devil's temptations made me realise how much he had spent his youth armed with God's Word.

I wanted to study medicine and I was very jealous of my friends who were studying at Seoul National University. I studied hard, but I didn't have the grades to get into Seoul National University, so I was always worried. It was almost impossible with my abilities, so I prayed to Jesus because I believed in the Bible, which said that if you believe and ask, you will receive. But Jesus didn't answer me. I even blamed God.

"Why wasn't I born with the ability to get into Seoul National University?"

I also have a mother. She worked to feed her son and send him to school. There was a bank next to Mokchok Bridge in Daejeon, and my mother set up a small shop on the corner of the bank. It was more of a temporary building than a shop. It was about the size of a kiosk on the street today.

It was next to the bank for a reason. Although we now do our financial transactions online, everyone used to cycle to the bank to do their business. The main purpose of the shop was to protect the bikes. The bank allowed us to operate on the condition that we protected our customers' bikes. So when customers parked their bikes on the rack, we would go out and hang a number plate on the handlebars of the bikes, and the other one would be kept by the customer, and then they would go to the bank to settle their accounts. Even if we kept our eyes open, sometimes the bikes would be stolen and we would be charged the full value of the bikes.

In the shop, my father worked as a bike guard and my mother had a sewing machine and she worked on glued-on fabric with window tint to make name badges for students and soldiers. During the back-to-school season, we had a lot of group orders for name badges, which kept us up at night trying to meet delivery deadlines.

One night I went to bed and didn't hear my sewing machine, I heard a moan from somewhere. I got out of bed to find my mother had a bandage on her finger and was using a red medicine called Mercurochrome to ease the pain. On a normal sewing machine you need a presser foot to move the needle, but you can't use a presser foot when you're engraving a name badge. So the tips of your index fingers act as the presser foot, and the sewing machine needle moves up and down with the power of the motor to engrave the name badge. That day, after a few sleepless nights, my mother was engraving name tags. In the blink of an eye, the needle had sewn through my mother's finger.

My father loved his children and his wife as much as anyone. He opened the nameplate shop next to the bank because it was a good business location, and he was allowed to do so on the condition that he looked after the bicycles of the customers who came to the bank, but he didn't get paid by the bank. The only source of income was the badge shop. Once the badge shop was doing well, he started supplying trinkets such as soldiers' badges and rank insignia. Nowadays, soldiers and government officials are pretty clean, but back then, ceremonial payments and bribes were common on delivery days. My father made a point of bribing the inspectors with alcohol, which became so common that he became an alcoholic.

Nobody in my family believed in Jesus. My father would come home drunk and on those days he would turn into a crazy person. Once he started drinking too much, he was no longer a normal person. On the days when he came home drunk, he would wake up the rest of the family. I was so afraid of my father who was turning into a madman.

A Family of Horrors (2005)

The Bible says, "Be sober" (Ephesians 5.18), which means we should not allow the devil to control us. When my father believed in Jesus and stopped drinking, he had already had a stroke. He was in the hospital for a long time before he died. After my father died, the demon of alcohol entered my brother's body and whenever he drank too much, he acted like a crazy person. Finally, my brother ended his life by committing suicide. I fell into a deep pit of despair as I looked at my broken family.

I didn't know what on earth I was going to do. Since my father's death, my family's business had become a shadow of its former self. It felt as if my family's traditions and heritage had been completely lost. The poverty was bearable to a certain extent, but handing over the spirit of my family to the devil and surrendering to him was unacceptable. I decided to entrust my mother, sisters and younger brothers to God to take control of our lives.

And now I find that a new power is moving in me. I find that the Holy Spirit of God is alive and well in me because I trust in God's work at work in me. Now there is a new power moving in me. I must confess that the life I have been living according to my own will, guided by the world, only leads to a dead end in life, but those who pay attention to God are led to a life that is open and wide, free and full.

CHAPTER 2
WORLDLY WISEMAN

My childhood was not a very prosperous one, and I have no doubt that I am much better off now than I was then. But I do not consider myself happy, because I have a pathetic feeling that I am merely watching my neighbors suffer. On my pilgrimage I meet people who are too proud and too well-off, and among them are those who, armed with worldly knowledge, tempt me into the "swamp of despair." That is why I could not have come this far without the help of an evangelist.

When Christian left the city of destruction, there was one person who followed him: Obstinate and Pliable. Obstinate stopped Christian and asked him why he had left his hometown. Christian replied, "I am going in search of an inheritance that is undefiled and unfading in heaven, and I want you to enjoy this unimaginable treasure and be blessed by accompanying me. As long as you remain here, you will not escape destruction; so it is written so in this book I have."

Obstinate (center) and Pliable (right)

But Obstinate eventually rejected Christian's advice and returned to the city of destruction, because the field of his heart was by the wayside, according to the biblical parable of the sower (Matt. 13:4). He was a man whose heart had already been hardened by his own stubbornness, a man whose heart had already been hardened to receive the word of God. Pliable that accompanied Obstinate overcame Obstinate's recommendation to return to the city of destruction, and he agreed with Christian, declaring,

"I will share my destiny with Christian."

But Pliable's companionship did not last long: walking carelessly along the road, he fell into a "bog of despair" in the middle of a field. As he struggled to get out, he shouted to Christian

> "Do you mean to tell me that this is the happy life you promised me for this pilgrimage?"

And then he turned and ran back the way he had come, never looking back. Christian barely made it out of the swamp, thanks to the "help" of an evangelist who happened to be passing by. Christian asked the evangelist for help to save him.

"Sir, I heard that this road leads to the narrow gate of the city of destruction, so why don't you fix this pothole on the way?" The helper replied

> "This deep quagmire cannot be repaired, and that is why it is called the quagmire of discouragement. When sinners realise their hopeless condition, all kinds of fears, doubts and despairs arise in their hearts, and they all flow into this place and accumulate there, so it always remains a bad place".

Swamp of despair(2022)

After being lifted out of the morass of discouragement by a helping hand, Christian met a new person: Worldly Wiseman. He approached me up to Christian and asked him.

"How come you are carrying such a heavy burden on your back with such a poor mule, and where are you going?"

Christian replied, "I'm listening to the evangelist and I'm going toward the wicket gate."

Worldly Wiseman said he would lead you to an easy and safe way where you could lay down your heavy burden, pointing to the hilltop 'Moral Village'.

"When you get there," he said, "you'll meet 'The Law Guru', and he'll lighten the heavy burden on Christian's shoulders. If he's out riding, meet his son, 'Courtesy.'"

Although he was kindly showing Christian the way, Worldly Wiseman was actually compromising with a world that did not recognise the ransom work of Jesus Christ and put ethics and social reform before the Gospel. He was tempting Christian by offering to show him a comfortable, easy way to go instead of the difficult pilgrimage.

Christian took Worldly Wiseman's advice and set out in search of the village, but the road to it was steep and the path was very rough. The burden he was carrying began to feel much heavier. Suddenly, he saw a fire roaring up the hill, and he feared that if he climbed it, he would be consumed by the flames and burn to death. He began to sweat and tremble with fear.

Eventually, Christian began to regret following the wrong advice of Worldly Wiseman. Luckily, he was able to find the help who rescued him from his despondency and showed him the way back to the wicket gate.

Christian at the entrance to Moral Village (2022)

Academic Worldly Wisemen

While attending church, I have encountered Worldly Wisemen in my academic world, first Charles Darwin of the theory of evolution and then Richard Dawkinson, author of The Selfish Gene. Charles Darwin believes that our ancestors evolved from chimpanzees. He argues for evolution by natural selection. But the Bible has a different answer.

It says, 'In the beginning God created man, in the image of God he created him (Genesis 5:1). No one has ever seen God.' (John 1:18; 1 John 4:12).

If God created man according to these words, then it seems clear that God's Spirit of providence, not evolution, created man.

What did Darwin mean by natural selection? Darwin used the term artificial selection to describe the different breeds of domesticated animals, such as dogs, of which there are more than 350 breeds. He explained this by saying that humans had deliberately created the breeds.

So who was involved in species diversity?

Darwin explains the idea of the diversity of species in this world with the concept of natural selection. From the point of view of faith and spirituality, it seems clear that the diversity of life on earth was created by the invisible One, the One who?

Richard Dawkinson argues that altruism, the biblical command to "love your neighbor as yourself" (Matthew 19:19), is also a manifestation of selfish genes. He goes so far as to argue that humans are mere carriers of genes, that there never was a God, and that this is an "invented God delusion.

The Academic Worldly Wisemen (2022)

God = Spirit

The Bible says, "God is light (1 John 1:5)," and the term light appears 196 times. In modern physics, light is called a tiny particle of energy (a photon). In biology, light is also the source of life, used in photosynthesis. When we say light, these tiny particles are moving. The speed of light is about 300,000 kilometers per second. There is nothing in the world that is faster than that, and if somebody could cut that tiny particle traveling 300,000 kilometers per second with a sharp knife, it would turn into something that doesn't exist. This is what the Bible calls the Spirit of God.

> 'In the beginning God created the universe, the earth was formless and desolate. The raging ocean that covered everyting was engulfed in total darkness, and the Spirit of God was moving over the waters' (Genesis 1:1-2).

Isaiah describes God's spirit as 'a life-giving spirit, a spirit of wisdom and understanding, a spirit of direction and strength, a spirit that inspires knowledge and the fear of God.' (Isa. 11:2-3).

God is not, in the words of Worldly Wisemen and zoologist Richard Dawkinson, 'a made god'. As a natural scientist, I have written and painted to testify that 'there is a God'. Jesus came to earth as the Son of God. This is how he introduced himself.

> "I am the way, the truth, and the life; no one goes to the Father except by me" (John 14:6).

The God who calls us to be the way, the truth, and the life calls us by name, whereas the storks and animals I study call us by number.

'God doesn't count us; He calls us by name. Arithmetic is not His focus (Romans 9:27, The Message).

God is beyond the concept of time. If time exists for God, it is only in the present moment, and even that moment is gone before we can finish saying that "now" is the present moment. One of the difficulties that arises when we trap God in the concept of time is that He is not a temporal being. As Christians, we all believe that "God knows what we're going to do tomorrow," but if God really knows what I'm going to do tomorrow, don't I have the freedom to act differently?

This is the difficulty that arises when we imprison God in our concept of time, the difficulty that arises when we think that God is different from us because He knows what's ahead, because we characterize Him as a being who lives by our concept of time.

If God could foresee our actions, it would be very difficult to believe that we have freedom of action. But if we think of God as timeless and beyond time. He can see the day we call 'tomorrow' as 'today'. For God, every day is just 'now.'

God, who existed as spirit in the beginning, came to earth in the incarnation of Jesus, and before He died on the cross, He said.

"If I do not go away, the Holy Spirit will not come to you. But if I go away, I will send the Holy Spirit to come to you (John 16:7)."

According to this statement, Jesus, the Messiah, is already in me, because the Holy Spirit, the Comforter, is with me now, transcending the concept of time. As I read through the Bible, one passage stands out as a reminder that God is timeless.

> "For to the Lord a day is as a thousand years, and a thousand years as a day." (2 Peter 3:8)

Given Peter's confession, it is clear that God has no concept of time and is beyond it. He interferes with human beings who live in the concept of time only in Spirit.

There are miracles in the Bible that are incomprehensible to us humans who live within the concept of time. For example, in the Gospel of John (2:1-10), Jesus goes to a wedding feast in Cana of Galilee and performs the miracle of turning water into wine. When you look at it in terms of time, you have to have grapes and ferment them to make wine. It takes time to grow grapes and it takes time to ferment them to make wine, but this is an event that completely eliminates the concept of time: water turned into wine.

Jesus, as God, transcended the concept of time and performed a miracle. What Jesus foreshadowed for us through this event is the concept of time in heaven. Heaven, where we go after our physical death, is a place where there is no such concept as time.

An Evangelist on My Pilgrimage

There was a true evangelist who helped me walk with these heavy burdens. He was Elder Kim Yong-ki (1909-1988), the founder of Canaan Farming School in Gwangju, Gyeonggi-do, whom I met in college and who taught me how to live a Christian life of frugality, sweat and hard work.

At that time, Korean society was very bad. It was just after the end of the Korean War, so there was a shortage of living materials, and we received aid from the United States. At Canaan Agricultural School we were taught to put into practice the words of the Bible, "He who does not work should not eat!" (2 Thessalonians 3:10). To conserve resources, we were taught to use toothpaste sparingly, no more than the size of a small fingernail. They ate sweet potatoes for one of their three meals, now considered a snack, but then a staple food.

Elder Kim Yong-ki taught us how to live as Christians by working diligently and following the teachings of the Bible to get out of poverty. I think it is because of his teachings that Korea is living like this today.

Immediately after the May 16 Revolution, Park Chung-hee, chairman of the Supreme Council for National Reconstruction, attended Canaan Agricultural and Military School, where he received his education, became president, and then led the Saemaul movement for the people. After that, the modernization of Korea was like the miracle of Jesus' healing of the five loaves and two fishes in the Bible

The miracle of the five Breads and two fishes (2020)

Jesus said, "Make the people sit down" (John 6:10-13). The people took their seats and sat down, and there were about five thousand people. Jesus took the loaves, blessed them, and distributed them to the seated. He did the same with the fish. Then the people were filled and had twelve kilograms left over.

All those present were amazed, for this could not have been done except by God.

"This is surely the prophet. God's prophet has come right here to Galilee!"

As the crowd cheered enthusiastically, Jesus realized that they wanted to seize him and make him king, so he fled the scene and went back up the mountain.

How can we interpret this miracle of Jesus?

On the one hand, it's a miracle that fills the bellies of a poor people, but in the context of our current affluence, it also reads as a story about the value of the little guy and the little things. In our modernised age we love the big, the many, the large and the complicated. God chooses the small things that are often ignored in this hard and complicated age. The five barley loaves and two fish that the little boy has are just that: small. Through the miracle of the five loaves and two fishes we realise that in the hands of the Lord they are multiplied. When we share small gifts with the little ones, God's generous grace is revealed.

Faith without actions

I leave my house to get some lunch. I leave my house and find a subway station, and at the entrance to the subway station there is an old man selling "Big Issue" magazines. All the old men selling "Big Issue" magazines are known to be homeless. The magazine costs 7,000 won, and when they sell it, they get 3,500 won back. When I heard this, I decided to have a cheap lunch, because I wanted to save money on lunch and buy the magazine during my pilgrimage.

There's a man who comes around every few weeks. It's the man who sells Big Issue magazines at the entrance to the subway station. But on this day, he was nowhere to be seen. Was he ill? Or had he stopped selling because the magazines weren't selling?" I looked around, wondering what was going on.

In the same place where he was selling the Big Issue, a mother and daughter in black long puffers were selling bundles of socks. At first I walked past them, but when I returned from a quick post run, I saw a white boxy car parked on the side of the road. Apparently, business wasn't going well, so they folded up their stall and loaded the socks into the car. I don't know what made them decide to sell socks.

The sight of the mother and daughter reminded me of my own mother engraving name tags for her mom's mom-and-pop roadside shop, which was normal back then when you couldn't afford it, but now it seemed so foreign. By the time I decided to run over and buy her a few pairs of socks, she was long gone.

I felt guilty that I had failed to live out the Lord's command to "love thy neighbour". The Bible teaches that "faith without action is not true love. This teaching is made clear in the following verses

> "My brethren, what good is it for someone to say that he has faith if his actions do mot prove it? Can that faith save him" (James 2:14).

Today, I had no choice but to walk this pilgrimage again with heavy steps, unable to lift my head before God. I had double-checked the 10,000 won bill in my wallet, knowing that the next time I saw that mother and daughter, I would run over and buy them a pair of socks.

CHAPTER 3

THE WICKET GATE

I was reluctant to enter the wicket gate, perhaps because I had a lingering sense that I had to let go of the things of this world, but I had no choice if this was the path to the City of Zion, and on this way I had to let go of the storks that I considered most precious. Just as Christian walked through the wicket gate and stood on the hill of the cross, I realise that I am on a spiritual journey aboard this ship called Earth that God has made from the beginning of time.

When Christian realised that the Moral Village was a city of worldly people, led him to the wicket gate.

How long did he walk?

Finally, Christian reached the wicket gate. Without hesitation, Christian knocked on the narrow door and 'Good Will' opened the door and asked.

"Are you looking for someone?" he asked again.

"Yes, I'm fleeing from the city of destruction and making my way to Mount Zion. Do you accept sinners like me?"

To this Christian's question, Goodwill answered this Christian's question with all his heart.

He said, "All that the Father gives me will come to me, and whoever comes to me I will never cast out." (John 6:37)

At the Wicket gate (2022)

Goodwill drew him to the door again and said.

"Come in," he said, "for not far from this gate is Beelzebub's citadel, where he shoots arrows to stop pilgrims who pass through this gate. But don't worry, you can now take the narrow but straight path you see before you. It was paved by the forefathers of our faith. Look ahead. Do you see the narrow path stretching out before you? That is the path you must take from now on, the path that was made by your forefathers, many prophets, by Christ and by his disciples, a path that is as straight as if it had been marked with a ruler, and that is the path you must take from now on."

Christian's questions and well-intentioned answers follow.

"This burden I am carrying is so heavy, is there any way I can get rid of it?"

"Though your burden is heavy, carry it until you reach the place of salvation. When you get there, your burden will fall from your back by itself."

With that, Christian fastened his belt and said goodbye to his good intentions.

Christian being led by goodwill up the path to Mount Zion (2022)

A stork through a narrow door

I am a natural scientist who has tried to restore the extinct Oriental Stork (an internationally protected bird of the first class of endangered species) in my country. In my life's pilgrimage, I once flew to the Amur River in Russia to collect the birds that still exist in nature, and after 15 years of hard work in the laboratory of a university where I was a professor, I succeeded in breeding storks. In 2015, we released the first 10 storks back into the wild in my country. After I retired from the university, the storks were transferred to the responsibility of the head of a local government organisation, and they are released indiscriminately into the wild every year.

The general majority thinks that releasing storks into nature is restoration, and they claim it is, so now, year after year, storks are being released into nature as they think they should. I scream that it shouldn't be done, but they don't listen. The majority is not always the right way. Without the restoration of biodiversity and in our country, the storks will not live out their lives and will disappear. I often feel sorry for the storks I brought in from Russia, bred and released into the wild. I want to help them, but the majority thinks differently, so I have decided to lay down my stork burden.

If there's one political system that modern humans have found to be the best, it's probably democracy, and as postmoderns, we've come to accept the idea that the majority is always right as a matter of course, but that majority thinking doesn't apply to everything.

When Copernicus published his theory that the earth was round and revolved around the sun, no one believed him. In retrospect, the view of majority view was proven wrong. The same is true of stork restoration in Korea. Stork restoration is a research project, but many people don't see it that way, and that's why it's so difficult. I always feel that the sacrifice of the storks is inevitable.

If storks used to breed and live in Korea, it was before I was born, and there are few records of how they used to breed and live in Korea. As a natural scientist, I wanted to find out where the storks came from in the past and how they had lived in the Land of the Rising Sun. As a natural scientist, I came up with the following hypothesis.

"Before the Korean people lived on the Korean peninsula, they bred in the marshes along the Amur River in Russia. They found a beautiful wetland in an eastern country, and one or two began to settle there. The storks flew to the villages where people were cultivating rice fields, built nests in the trees of the houses, and lived there, breeding, and the storks flew south with their grown chicks. The Yangtze River in China was probably their wintering area. Of course, after the winter, they would fly back to the Korean peninsula to breed and live like this for thousands of years. But one day, humans began to clear farmland and spray pesticides to increase agricultural production, and their meat-based diet polluted the farmland with the waste water from livestock. In addition, the Korean War destroyed the stork nests in the flames of bombing raids. Thus, the stork, which had lived for thousands of years, disappeared from the land in less than 100 years.

The Korean Stork's Nest (2019)

Stork restoration for the sake of storks, or simply releasing storks into the wild, is not true stork restoration. God created this earth in the beginning with an interest in people, one person at a time. He calls creatures like storks by their numbers, but He treats people differently - He calls them by our names.

That is why I was so interested in the stork restoration project. On the field where the farmers live, I was focused on improving the quality of life of the people. But when it came to breeding storks, I found that there was no one who agreed with my idea. In the end, the narrow gate for me was the restoration of storks in this country.

An escaped stork

It was the spring of 2014 when a two-year-old female stork escaped from the aviary we managed(Cheongwon-gun, Chungcheongbuk-do). We named her Miho, after the local river. It's more accurate to say that Miho disappeared than than escaped, as she slipped through an open door during a brief moment when the zookeepers were feeding her and was gone in a flash.

Seven months later, in the winter, I received a tip that Miho had been seen in Hadong, Gyeongnam. The tipster alerted me after seeing a name tag attached to Miho's leg. In the early spring of the following year, Miho returned to Baekgokcheon in Jincheon, Chungcheongbuk-do, not far from the captive storks. Jincheon was one of the breeding grounds for storks in Korea's past. If my hypothesis was correct, she was trying to breed there. It was one day in May. Miho lasted less than three months there due to pesticide poisoning and disappeared, never to be seen again.

How did we know it was pesticide poisoning?

It was farming season, and I saw a neighbor nearby spraying herbicide, claiming it was for the grass. Also, the grass had already turned yellow there where Miho had flown, and there were empty pesticide bottles lying around.

This reminded me of Noah's Ark: when God judged the earth with water, the first thing Noah did was to send a raven outside to see if the water had receded. Noah's experiment resulted in a dove. Just as he knew the water had receded when he saw the dove come back with an olive leaf in its beak, so he knew it wasn't time to send his storks out yet.

Noah's Ark was an event in the place where God judged the earth with water. Humans had polluted the land with pesticides, herbicides, animal sewage, and livestock manure, making it a land where even storks had no place to roost.

The Sound of Silence

The first animal I encountered after becoming a naturalist was a bat. The first time I heard a bat's ultrasound through a bat detector, I was excited about my research because I was hearing sounds I hadn't heard with my own ears in my entire life. Bats use ultrasound to find food and detect obstacles. Even the vampire bats I did my dissertation on communicate with each other by sending and receiving ultrasonic waves.

When I first heard them with my ultrasonic detector, they came to me like an orchestra playing. As a moth flapped its wings in the distance and approached, the echoes changed pitch rapidly, rising and falling almost an octave apart. The bat was using sound to see a world that seemed frozen in time, a world that seemed to be a series of compartmentalized movements, like people dancing in the middle of the night with strobes (flashing lights) on. I was in awe of the ecology of the bat and thought, "Ah, God made these sounds in the beginning!" Long before humans walked the earth. The Bible records these natural mysteries.

"What no one ever saw or heard, what no one ever thought could happen, is the very thing God prepared for those who love him" (1 Corinthians 2:9).

Silence in the Dark (2015)

Our planet, the Earth, revolves around the sun at a speed of nearly 30 kilometers per second. That's over 100,000 kilometers per an hour, and the sound it makes is an ultrasonic squeal hundreds of thousands of times louder than the ultrasound of a bat. It's a good thing, because if we could hear it, no one would be alive on this planet.

Inside the cochlea of the human ear is a very thin basilar membrane that vibrates with frequency. If you stretch it out, it's less than 3 centimeters long. The entrance to the cochlea detects low frequencies and the tip of the cochlea detects only 20,000 Hz high frequencies. Ultrasound is anything above 20,000 hertz, which is why we don't hear the ultrasound of a bat or the sound of the earth spinning. God designed and created us from the ground up to not to be able to hear sounds that obviously exist in this universe but are above the threshold of basilar membrane vibration.

A Spaceship, the Earth

In the beginning, God created the first plants and animals in a spaceship called Earth, and then He created the first passenger, Adam. But then many of the passengers ignored the invisible God and made their own idols to worship as their gods. That wasn't all; they also fell prey to Satan's deception of sin, which led to death. Eventually, mankind was reduced to a futile existence of wrestling in the mud.

From that point on, God chose to mold the lives of those who love Him into the pattern of the life of His Son, Jesus. The Son of God sits in the front row cockpit of these passengers whom He has restored (Romans 8:28-29). The pilot of this ship is God, and the one holding the controls to His right is His only begotten Son, Jesus.

Having just walked through the narrow door, "I," a Christian, boarded a spaceship called Earth. A flight attendant leads him to a seat marked with a cross and takes the heavy burden he's been carrying on his back. Christian couldn't have been happier relieved of the sin that had been weighing him down, and he shouted for joy.

"Because the Lord came in the flesh and suffered like us, I have rest, and because he chose death for himself, I have life!" The second flight attendant approached Christian, who kindly took off his dirty clothes and put on a new one. Christian thought of a Bible verse.

'The angel said to his heavenly attendants, "Take away the filthy garments that this man is wearing." Then he said to Joshua, "I have taken away your sin and will give you new clothes to wear.' (Zech. 3:4)

The apostle Paul also advised in Ephesians, 'Put off the old man and put on the new man' (4:22-24).

The third crew member approached Christian and placed a seal on his forehead. He then handed him a tightly sealed scroll and told him to open it often during this space voyage. At this point, Christian was reminded of another Bible verse.

> 'And you also became God's people when you heard the true message, the good news that Christ brought, and God put his stamp of the Holy Spirit he had promised. (Eph. 1:13).'

He decided to take out the scroll and read it from time to time as he traveled in his spaceship here on earth. Oh, and he wasn't the only Christian on board. An amazing 8 billion people were on board.

The Spaceship, Earth (2021)

CHAPTER 4

THE INTERPRETER'S HOUSE

Everyone needs a mentor to help them succeed in life. This is especially true if you are a person of faith who aspires to heaven. Christian had an "interpreter". The Interpreter told Christian a story that he needed to take to heart on his pilgrimage to Zion...

Christian's body felt lighter after he had shed his heavy burden. He held a scroll in his hand. Arriving at the Interpreter's house, accompanied by a "benevolent" guide, Christian described himself as follows.

"I am a stranger from the city of destruction, and I have come because someone who knows the master of this house told me to come here and see the master of this house, and he will show me something profitable. Is the master of this house inside?"

After the porter went to call for the Master, the interpreter appeared. Christian greeted him politely.

"I am a pilgrim traveling from the City of Destruction to Mount Zion. I was told that you would show me some useful things that would help me on my pilgrimage, so I have come.

"You have come to the right place, I will show you things that will help you.

Christian was very grateful for the interpreter's kindness. The interpreter told his servant to light a candle and asked Christian to follow him.

Interpreter and Christian (2022)

The Waterer and the Broom

The interpreter took him to a very large room that had never been cleaned and was covered with dust. As the servant began to clean the room, Christian was nearly suffocated by the amount of dust. "Bring some water over here and sprinkle it," he said to a woman standing next to him. As she did, the dust settled and the room became clean. "This room has been sanctified by the sweet grace of the gospel," the interpreter explained.

"This room represents a human heart that has never been sanctified by the sweet grace of the gospel. The dirt represents man's original sin and the corruption that makes every human being that way. The man who first began to sweep this room is the law; the woman who next watered it is the gospel. The law identifies sin and forbids it, but it doesn't eradicate it. Just as the woman sprinkled water on the floor and all the dirt settled, so sin is covered and eradicated. Likewise, when our souls are cleansed by faith, they are transformed into "a place fit for the King of glory to dwell.

The waterer and the broom (2022)

Soon after, the interpreter took Christian's hand and led him to another small room where two boys named "Desire" and "Patience" were sitting.

"Why is Desire angry?"

This time the interpreter was kind enough to answer.

"The boys' father told them to wait until the beginning of next year because he would bring them their favorite presents, but Desire wanted them now and Patience was willing to wait. But then he saw a man come up to Desire with a bag of treasure and pour it out at her feet. Desire picked it up and squandered it at will, enjoying it and laughing and mocking at Patience; but in a short time Desire had squandered it all, and all that was left was a ragged piece of rags.

Desire and Patience

"What does that mean?"

Christian asked again, and the interpreter replied.

"These two boys are symbolic figures. Desire symbolizes people in this world, and patience symbolizes people in the next world. As we have just seen, desire wants to have everything in this world right now. Similarly, the people of this world want to have everything they can get their hands on now, and they can't wait for the world to come, so the saying, "A bird in the hand is better than two in the forest," is considered more trustworthy to them than God's testimony of the bliss of the world to come. But just as lust, as you can see, squandered everything in an instant and had nothing left but a scrap of rags, so will all those whose eyes are darkened by the things of this world end up like him when the end of this world comes.

Passion and Patience (2022)

Anointing and sprinkling with water

The interpreter took Christian's hand again and led him into another room where a fire was burning in a fireplace. A man stood by the fireplace and threw a lot of water on it to put out the flames, but instead of going out, the fire burned higher and higher and hotter.

"What does this mean?"

Christian asked.

"This fire represents grace at work in a person's heart. It is the devil who tries to extinguish the fire by throwing water on it, but the fire still burns more and more intensely. Now I will show you why.

As he said this, the interpreter took the Christian to the back of the wall, where a man with a jar of oil in his hand was secretly but steadily pouring oil on the fire. The interpreter continued.

"This is the Christ. He is constantly anointing human hearts with the oil of grace to preserve the grace He has already placed in them. No matter how hard the devil tries to take away grace, human souls will always enjoy His merciful favor because of Him, and the fact that He is standing behind the wall, as you can see, constantly anointing the fire to keep it burning, teaches you how difficult it is to keep that grace alive in a soul once it has fallen into the devil's deception."

Christian said, "Thank you so much for teaching me so many good things. Now, I think it's time for me to go."

Anointing and Sprinkling (2022)

The Interpreter I Met

For a Christian, an interpreter is someone who strengthens his faith. On my pilgrimage, I have an interpreter in the apostle Paul, who was not originally a believer in Jesus. In fact, he was the one who imprisoned and persecuted those who believed in Jesus. The day he was blinded on the road to Damascus and heard the voice of Jesus himself, he was on his way to hunt down the Christians. In the Bible, we see the transformation of Paul into a believer in Jesus.

On that day, Paul was on his way to the high priest to get an arrest warrant to take to the various synagogues in Damascus. As he reached the outskirts of Damascus, he was suddenly struck by a dazzling light. He fell to the ground and a voice called out to him.

Paul in Damascus (2022)

"Saul, Saul, why do you want to harm me?"
Lord, who are you?
"I am Jesus, whom you are persecuting." (Acts 9:1-5)

Paul lived a life of obedience to God from his conversion to his martyrdom.

No one is free from sin and death. Originally, we were created without sin, but sin entered through Adam and we had to experience separation from God. Adam, who brought us into this situation, also points to the One who will deliver us from it (Romans 5:12-14). But this gift of salvation does not compare to the sin that brought death. Think about it: If the sin of one man pushed countless others into the abyss of death, separation from God, what does this gift of God, poured out through one man, Jesus Christ, bring us?

In a nutshell, just as one person did something wrong and brought us all into the predicament of sin's death, another person did something right and brought us all out of it (Romans 5:18-19). Sin is no match for that militant forgiveness we call grace. When sin and grace face off, it's always grace that wins. All sin can do is threaten us with death, and now that's over, because God is setting everything right through the Messiah, and grace brings us into life, into a life that never ends, into a world that never runs out (Romans 5:20-21)."

I'm not very moved by most pastors' sermons, probably because I'm too habitual a believer in Jesus. But when I read the 13 letters of Paul, things are different. I can read them over and over again and they are fresh. Of the 13 letters, Romans is the one that has the power to guide me in my spiritual life.

The Rev. Eugene Peterson, author of The Message Bible, writes in his introduction to Romans.

'The event that split history into "before" and "after" and changed the world took place about thirty years before Paul wrote this letter. The event

– the life, death, and resurrection of Jesus – other took place in a remote corner of the extensive Roman Empire: the province of Judea in Palestine. Hardly anyone noticed, certainly no one in busy and powerful Rome. And when this letter arrived in Rome, hardly anyone read it, certainly no one of influence. There was much to read in Rome – imperial decrees, exquisite poetry, finely crafted moral philosophy – and much of it was world-class. And yet in no time, as such things go, this letter left all those writings in the dust. Paul's letter to the Romans has had a far larger inpact on its readers than the volumes of all those Roman writers put together.'

Truly, I would have lived in ignorance of God and His Son Jesus Christ if it weren't for Paul. When I awoke from my sleep, I reached for my Bible again. Peter is speaking to me today from 2 Peter 1:10-11 where he says

> "Prove that God was right in calling and choosing us, so that we may have life in the eternal kingdom of Jesus Christ."

Peter turns to me again in 2 Peter and asks me this.

I know that sooner or later I will die. What I especially want you to do is to write down all these things so that you can always look them up after I leave this world" (2 Peter 1:15, The Message).

I dare say my favorite Bible writer is Simon Peter. He didn't have the stellar resume that people have today; he didn't inherit the best intellect and superior genes of his day like Paul did; he wasn't a learned scholar; he was a fisherman; he only wrote two epistles, 1 and 2 Peter, but he couldn't have done it if God hadn't called him to it.

God chose people with great family DNA, like Paul, who were intelligent and learned, but He also chose people with humble DNA, like Peter, to be servants of Jesus. If there is any hope, it is that these writings of mine will be used as an instrument for good in the Lord, just as our forefathers in the faith were.

CHAPTER 5

SIMPLE·SLOTHFUL·PRESUMPTION.

We advise the lazy to emulate the industriousness of ants. But are ants really industrious? Ants aren't alone, and most animals aren't very industrious. The latest hot topic in biology is sociobiology. Ants have provided the basis for the study of sociobiology. Using sociobiological theories and ants, I would like to tell a story about the Lord who lives in me with a cast of characters: Simple, Slothful, Presumption, Formalist and Hypocrisy.

Simple (right) Slothful (center)
Presumption (left) (2022)

Christian, unburdened, found three men standing at the foot of a hill. Their wrists were shackled, and their names were Simple, Slothful, and Presumption.

"Hello," Christian said, "if you're willing, I'll try to untie your shackles."

Christian saw the suffocating condition of the three pilgrims and wanted to help them break free. But their responses were unexpected.

Simple: I don't feel any danger, just how good life is just the way it is.

Slothful: I'm just going to sit here and relax and chat.

Presumption: Everyone else is living their own lives. Why don't you stay out of everyone else's business and mind your own business.

Christian tried to help the three pilgrims who were in a spiritually dangerous situation, but their responses were met with apathy, laziness, and irritation. As Christian was about to say goodbye to them, he saw two people jumping over the wall to his left from the other side of the narrow street. One was labeled "Formalist" and the other was labeled "Hypocrisy. Christian went over to talk to them.

Formalist and Hypocrisy (2022)

"Where are you two coming from and where are you going?"

Christian's question was answered first by Formalist.

"We are from the city of vain glory, and we are on our way to Mount Zion to find glory."

Christian continued his question.

"There is a gate at the end of this street; why do you not enter through it, but go over the wall? Don't you know that it is written in the Bible that he who does not enter through the gate and goes over the wall to another place is a thief and a robber?

Then, this time, Hypocrisy answered.

"It's not just us, it's the people in my town who say that the way to Zion through the gate at the entrance is too far and too hard, so they all take a shortcut and climb over the wall like us"

Christian didn't back down.

"Wouldn't it be a sin to take such an illegal and easy way to violate the will of the Lord of the Heavenly Kingdom we are now seeking?

He is no fool either.

"There is no need for you to make a fuss about such things; this is a custom that has been practiced by the people of my hometown for more than a thousand years.

The Christian fires back.

"I am acting according to God's law, but you are acting as you please, aren't you? God, the owner of this road, declares that anyone who crosses the wall is a thief".

This time, Hypocrisy replies.

"When it comes to laws and regulations, we are just as conscientious as you are, so we are no different from you or us in that regard".

After this conversation, Formalist, Hypocrite, and Christian reached the base of Hill Difficult. Formalist and Hypocrisy chose a path that wrapped around the mountain to the left and headed back. It was a path of danger. It wasn't a straight path, as the name implies, but a complicated one that splintered into many different faiths. Hypocrisy, deciding that climbing the mountain would be much more work than he thought, took the path of destruction to the right. It, too, was not a straight path, but one that branched off into a thousand forks in pursuit of different faiths and social philosophies. But Christian took out the scroll given to him on the cross and began to read. He soon made up his mind and resumed the path the evangelist had taught him.

Spirituality from ants

It was John Bunyan's ingenious way of storytelling that led him to introduce the Simple, the Slothful, and the Presumptuous to the Christian pilgrimage. Through them he wanted to point out the spiritual laziness of the people of his time. You can read his thoughts in the original text, with occasional biblical commentary. The Bible directly advises us to look at ants and learn from them.

> Go to the ant, thou sluggard, and learn from what he does (Prov. 6:6)
>
> He prepares his food in the summer, and gathers his provisions in the harvest (Prov. 6:8).

We used to be told to watch ants or animals and learn wisdom from them. Before I studied animal behavior, I also thought that all animals were busy, except for those whose names are easily recognizable, such as sloths. But if you watch animals, you'll see that they spend most of the day resting, except when they're hunting. Nowadays, wildlife documentarians wait all day or even several nights to get a shot. I often felt bored as a researcher when I traveled with a documentary crew to the uninhabited breeding grounds of Hongdo Island in Gyeongnam Province to study the communication system between mother gulls and their offspring. Professor Edward O. Wilson, who first pioneered the field of Sociobiology with his research on ants, received his Ph.D. from Harvard University and worked there until his death in December 2021 at the age of 92. I was involved in the Korean translation of his massive book 'Sociobioloy, the New Synthesis' and marveled at the "unity of his biological insights, applied consistently from lower organisms to higher social organisms and then to human groups.

His sociobiology has had a tremendous impact beyond biology into sociology, cultural anthropology, ethics, and moral philosophy. Perhaps he could be a colleague of mine. I would be both envious and proud to have him as a colleague.

Today, scientists have discovered that within ant society, just as in human society, there are distinct occupations. Among other things, ants communicate primarily by smell. In ant societies, there are scavengers who take out the garbage. They do this grunt work all their lives. The scavengers smell like garbage. Other ants smell it and act aggressively. Even if the scavenger ants secretly want to do something else, they can't because of the garbage smell, because as soon as the other ants smell the garbage, they are drawn to the pile.

Also in the ant community are the funeral ants. These ants are particularly sensitive to the smell of oleic acid from a dead body. They don't check for breathing or a heartbeat to confirm life or death like humans do - they can tell when someone is dead just by smelling. It may be a little gross, but scientists do experiments by smearing oleic acid on the bodies of living ants. When the living ant smells oleic acid, it's dragged to the graveyard by other ants.

Ants (2021)

Humans have only been on this planet for 3 million years, but ants have been around for over 140 million years. And they don't get old for nothing-they've been around for over 100 million years longer than humans, so they've accumulated a whole civilization of their own experience.

We've identified 14,000 species of ants on this planet, and scientists estimate that there are probably many times that many more. They've occupied every part of the planet except Antarctica and the North Pole, so long before humans, each group has adapted to the Earth's soil and climate and built a civilisation.

Ants know how to use their caterpillars to make thin fabrics and how to use worker ants to provide food. We know how to turn ants into living refrigerators, breed aphids to squeeze out their secretions, and grow alcohol, flour and mushrooms.

When you climb a mountain, you can see the beauty and mystery of nature in the sky and on the ground. You can't help but marvel at the strange providence at work in these creatures with brains barely the size of a penny, and as scientists continue to explore, the land will continue to reveal more of the mysteries of these tiny creatures.

Having once lived as a scientist, I try to be a little more cheerful. When I realise that even this tiny life is working hard, I cry out to God's providence, who created a world without end long before humans lived on this earth.

An ant society that worships humans as gods

Could Professor Wilson have been influenced by his reading of The Ants?

In The Ants, French novelist Bernard Werber describes a cross-section of ant society that believes in humans as gods, and the novel's anti-Christian leanings are enough to intrigue readers with a penchant for the celestial, such as the characters 'Formalist' and 'Hypocrisy'.

The 'Gospel' spreads through the ant society, rendering them helpless as it spreads the circle sign, the symbol of their religion, which means 'finger'. The new queen of the ants is also very religious, so she slaughters the ants who believe in God. The end: More revered than any queen ant in ant history, many of the Finger Gods are willing to sacrifice themselves to help the Prophet Ant escape. When a giant earthworm stands in their way, he digs a small hole in its flank and places himself and his followers inside. The worm, which feels little pain, emerges to the surface where a giant chickadee eats it and ascends to heaven, where the ant and his followers die and ascend to the realm of the gods.

The novelist's imagination is also interesting from a scientific point of view. You might feel that the novel denigrates human beliefs by introducing an ant society, but when you actually observe ants, you realise that it's quite possible.

I'm at the top of Mt. Inwang, looking across a vast expanse at the towering skyscrapers of Yeouido, the Namsan Tower, but the ants at my feet can't see such a spectacular view. It's not that they're blind; they have eyes that can only see contrasts or silhouettes of objects at close range.

There was an ant at my feet, exploring towards me. When I bent down and grazed the bottom of a rock with my fingernail, it turned and scurried away. Ants have hairs on their legs that sense vibrations. To the ant's leg hair senses, the vibration of my nail must have been perceived as thunder and lightning suddenly descending from the sky. In this context, the novelist's idea that humans are gods to the ant's sensory world is convincing, which is why it became a bestseller.

Human and ants (2021)

My colleague, Professor Wilson, is not religious. His idea of God is different from mine.

Why is that?

In Lee's book, "Will Believing in Jesus Make You Happy," there's a conversation between a father and daughter who want to know the name of a beautiful flower.

"If you want to know the name of a flower, ask it, 'What is your name?' One day the flower will tell you its name." The daughter didn't believe her father's story. But one day, as he walked down the street, he crouched down in front of the flower with his child. A group of people passed by, looked at the flower and said aloud, "Lily of the valley is so pretty."

That's when the author learned the name of the flower. Wilson never knew the name of that flower, and I'm the guy who's been squatting in front of that flower all my life wanting to know the name of that flower. As I was squatting in front of that flower, there was a man who walked by and told me the name of that flower. It was the Apostle Paul.

He makes me confess with my lips, "The life I now live is not my own, but the life I live by faith in the Son of God, who loved me and gave his life for me (Galatians 2:20). I would not give up this life. I would never exchange it for the life of a scientist who wins a Nobel Prize and lives with the respect and admiration of the world."

CHAPTER 6
THE HILL DIFFICULTY

There are good times in the world, and then there are times of trouble. In the face of trouble, Formalist and Hypocrisy turn back the way they came. That can be you, and it's a struggle that every person of faith faces.
There are times when I can't even see a single word of Scripture. Such a difficult time came to me when a stork that had been close to me died in a faraway land, and as I reflected on my feelings, I realised that there was no one in the world who would feel sorry for the stork's death.

After saying goodbye to Formalist and Hypocrisy, Christian met another pilgrim at a bend in the road. No sooner had Christian crossed the "difficulty of the hill" than he met two pilgrims coming the other way: Timorous and Mistrust. Timorous said, "How can we continue on this road when we encounter more and more dangers?" So he said he would rather return to the starting point. Meanwhile, Mistrust said that if he continued on this path, he would see a lion ahead.

"If we continue on this path, will we not end up as food for the lion?"

"Fearing the hardships they might face in the future, the two retraced their steps and took the wrong path.

Timorous and Mistrust (2022)

Unable to turn back to the city of destruction that would burn with brimstone and sulphur, Christian had no choice but to continue on his way. He continued up the steep, straight mountain path because Timorous and Mistrust realised that the way back was the way to destruction. He barely made it up the mountain on his hands and knees.

When he reached the top of the mountain, a large tree provided shelter. Christian nodded off briefly under the tree and fell into a deep sleep. He dropped the scroll he was holding in his hand.

Christian falls into a deep sleep

Then someone appeared to him, woke him up, and said.

"You sluggard, go to the ant and see what he does and gain wisdom."

Hearing the words of Proverbs 6:6, Christian jumped to his feet and began to climb, not stopping until he reached the top of the mountain. After a while, Christian reached into his chest to read the scroll for comfort, only to find that it was gone.

Christian was discouraged and at a loss for what to do. Not only could he find comfort in the words written there, but the scroll was his passport to the New Jerusalem. Christian stood there like a dazed man, staring into space.

He remembered that he had lost it when he had fallen asleep in the shelter of the pass. He knelt down on the spot and asked God to forgive him for his foolishness. The walk back to the shelter was heavy and painful for him, as he sighed and sobbed, wishing the earth would go away.

Pilgrims Resting Under a Tree (2022)

All the way to the shelter, Christian searched the ground, hoping to find the scroll that had brought him so much comfort on his journey.

Fortunately, the scroll was there, he exclaimed.

"What a foolish man I am to doze under a tree in broad daylight, let alone in the midst of danger and trouble! The master of the pass had built a shelter under a tree for pilgrims to rest their souls, but I was in a hurry to use it to rest my body; I am a poor man!"

The stork that awakened spirituality

I try to stay awake, but it often doesn't happen. Sometimes the words of the Bible just don't come to me, especially when the peace of the flesh comes, and I become complacent. But then there was a stork that woke me up. It was a stork named 'Sanhwang'.

The stork was released in Yesan-gun, Chungcheongnam-do, almost 50 years after the last stork lived in Gwanseong-ri, Saengguk-myeon, Eumseong-gun, Chungcheongbuk-do, so it was named after the 'San' in Yesan. The Sanhwang was not just any stork; it was a stork that held the key to proving a hypothesis for natural scientists.

The stork that woke me up (2017)

The story goes back to 2015, when the first stork was reintroduced (released) into the wild.

The stork was released in September at Yesan Stork Park in Chungnam, South Korea, along with nine of his companions. Three months after his release, he made it all the way to the coast of Shinan, Jeollanam-do. I was tracking his journey in real time with a radio transmitter on his back.

He was hunting for food in the mudflats near Uido Island off the coast of Shinan. The time he stopped hunting and started flying south was 9am on 24 November 2015. It was an overcast day with dark clouds in the sky.

Later that day, after 6pm, Sanhwang's call was picked up in the East China Sea, far from the mouth of the Yangtze River in China. Sanhwang was two years old and this was his first long-distance migration, so he was following the map imprinted in his genetic information from his ancestors to the wintering grounds of the Yangtze estuary. It's about 600 kilometres from the coast of Xin'an to the wintering grounds of the Yangtze estuary, but about 200 kilometres from the estuary, Sanhwang began to change course.

"Oh, this is not right!"

I realised there was something wrong with Sanhwang.

It was then that we started receiving real-time data from the National Weather Service. Sure enough, it was raining in Shanghai, China, and dark clouds were beginning to gather over the East China Sea, just in time for Sanhwang to start changing course. Sanhwang began to turn almost 90 degrees to the left, heading for the East China Sea, where there were no islands for Sanhwang to land on.

Sanwhang flying over the East China Sea (2015)

A day and a half after leaving the waters off Shin'an, the bird began beeping again from Okinoerabu Island, near Okinawa at the southern tip of the Japanese archipelago. By the time it reached the island, it had flown almost 1,007 kilometres without taking a sip of water.

By 7am on 26 November 2015, the calls were no longer being picked up, and while it's clear the stork was alive for the first 12 hours after arriving on the island, we began to wonder what happened to it after the calls stopped.

As a scientist, he first contacted Japanese stork experts and then travelled to Japan to explain how the stork had flown to Japan. After hearing his explanation, the Japanese scientists contacted the head of the Okinoerabu community organisation to find out where the stork was. The local TV station broadcast a story about the stork.

"A stork has arrived in this island village from Korea, so if anyone has seen it, please report it immediately".

The transmission continued even after the stork's dial tone was cut off. It must have been about a month later.

A man confessed that he had found a dead stork on an airport runway with blood on its head and had promptly incinerated it. I first heard about this from a report in the Japanese newspaper Yomiuri.

I sent an email to Okinoerabu Airport asking about the burning of the stork. In Japan, storks are protected as natural monuments and special natural monuments, so burning them is illegal under the Cultural Property Protection Law. I filed a complaint with the Kagoshima Prosecutors Office against the airport staff who burned it.

I really wanted to know how Sanwhang survived and adapted to life on an island he had never been to before. If Sanwhang had survived, I would have submitted a paper to an international ornithological journal following his behaviour.

A year after I filed my complaint, the Kagoshima Public Prosecutor's Office sent me a notice of non-prosecution without investigating the perpetrators of the illegal incineration. As a scientist, I felt humiliated. Normally, the government, such as the Ministry of Foreign Affairs or the Agency for Cultural Affairs, would take action in such matters, but no one in my country took an active role.

"Is my country really sovereign?" I thought to myself.

When I came to this realisation, I was so overwhelmed that I broke down and cried.

The incident still left me with many doubts. The reason for my suspicion that the bird had been shot and not illegally burned was found in the death certificate sent to me by the airport, which stated.

"On the tarmac we found a body lying on the ground bleeding from a head wound caused by a landing airliner and immediately sent it to the incinerator.

That's not all, the pilot of the plane that day also sent me a message saying that he had seen a dead body on landing. I asked him to send me a picture of it, because if that was the case, there should have been a crash mark or something on the plane somewhere. But there was nothing on the plane in the picture he sent me. When that was the end of the airport's explanation, I couldn't help but become even more suspicious.

By the time Sanhwang arrived at the airport, he had not eaten for 34 hours and was probably extremely tired. It's easy to imagine what happened to him that day.

Okinoerabu Island has no rice paddies, and most of the agricultural land is used to grow sugar cane, so Sanwhang couldn't have found any wetlands to feed on. The only place he could have found was the lush grass around the airstrip, and as he scrambled to catch grasshoppers, he heard a shot fired in the distance. He jumped in surprise, but he couldn't have got very far - he was already exhausted.

Then the morning light broke, and just before the wheels of the plane's fuselage slid down the runway, a second bullet pierced the stork's head. The downed stork was thought to be an unusual bird by airport staff, who must have been terrified when they noticed the radio transmitter attached to its back. An affidavit from an airport employee who burned the bird without informing the authorities says: "I didn't realise it was a stork.

A stork at Okinoerabu Airport (2016)

I wanted to learn something new from him, and I wanted to find out what my predecessors hadn't found out. His death was a time of suffering, which I tell you about in the Bible.

And he strengthened the hearts of the disciples, exhorting them to continue in this faith, knowing that we must go through many tribulations if we are to enter the kingdom of God (Acts 14:22).

The apostle Paul also comforted us in the book of Romans.

The Holy Spirit helps us in our weakness. We do not even know how to pray, but the Spirit himself intercedes for us with groans that cannot be uttered (Romans 8:26).

As I continue this pilgrimage with the rest of the storks, I will try to take heart again.

God's thoughts versus my thoughts

What does God think about my efforts to reintroduce oriental-storks to the Korea? I am currently working on an ecological restoration project on the Korean Peninsula. Am I living a life with God?

The Bible (Hebrews 9:15, The Message) says: 'Christ offered himself as an unblemished sacrifice, freeing us from all those dead-end efforts to make ourselves respectable, so that we can live all out for God.'

It also says 'to have faith is to be sure of the things we hope for, to be cetain of the things we cannot see.' (Hebrews 11:1),and goes on to recount the stories of our ancestors who lived by faith. 'They were recognised as great people because of their faith.' By restoring the stork, I hope to become an ancestor of faith, as described in the Bible. The Bible mentions Abel, Enoch, Noah, Abraham and others as examples of this. They didn't act to make themselves great; God recognised their faith and saw them as complete people.

This is so true. I confess that, over the years, I have made pointless efforts to be great in my own right. I want to embark on my next pilgrimage with the intention of devoting myself entirely to God.

CHAPTER 7

A BEAUTIFUL HOUSE

Where there is hardship, there is also spiritual beauty. I received a priceless gift from God in a beautiful house in Germany. At every meal I ate directly from the life of the Lord; it was a moment of realization that I had the eternal life of the living Lord within me, which went beyond gratitude for the daily bread.

In the novel, Christian also stayed in a beautiful spiritual home where he found "prudence," "piety," and "charity" that he had not encountered on his pilgrimage. Let's take a look at the story of the beautiful home where Christian stayed, so rested and spiritually armed.

Christian hastened his journey to the beautiful house to spend the night. When he arrived at the beautiful house, Christian knocked on the door.

"Hello?"

The doorman came out and greeted Christian, and a conversation ensued.

"May I ask what brings you here?"

"Yes, can I stay here for the night?"

"The people here are here to support you and give you strength. Please come in."

"I lost my scroll on the way here, and I'm trying to find it, so I'm here late at night."

"Then I will call the lady of the house."

When Christian finished his conversation with the doorkeeper, he was greeted by three maidens: Prudence, Piety, and Charity.

They spent the rest of the day asking Christian questions, and he answered them faithfully.

Prudence Greets Christian the Pilgrim (2020)

"How did you come to leave your home and come this way?"

"I was so afraid that everything around me was going to be destroyed. I'm just so thankful that the evangelist told me about the wicket gate that I came this way. If it wasn't for him, I probably wouldn't have found this way.

"Don't you ever think about the city of destruction?"

"I think about it often. But I'm ashamed of it. I'm afraid I'll never be free of the thoughts of the world. I'm just grateful that these worldly thoughts are a shame to me, that they are no longer a pleasure. My joy now is to look toward the kingdom that has been promised to me."

"Did you not have a wife? Why didn't she come with you?"

"I had a wife, but she couldn't let go of the world as she knows it; she thinks the things of the world make her happy."

"Did you do everything you could to bring her with you? Did you do anything to mislead her as to your motives?"

"No. I was very careful that all my words were spoken in love. What rather displeased my wife was how careful I was not to sin and that we should love all, even our enemies. She thought this was silly."

"I can't help it if your wife turned away because she hated your loving heart."

Christian finished his story, was treated to a delicious dinner, and rested peacefully for the night. In the morning they all woke up. After huddling together and talking some more, they allowed Christian to see the many curiosities preserved in the house before heading out.

First, they took Christian to the study, where they showed him some books that recorded events from a very long time ago.

Gideon, Barak, Samson, Samson, Jephthah, David, Samuel, and the prophets, all of whom had overthrown nations by acts of faith, administered justice, and received what was promised. They had withstood attacks of lions, fire, and swords; they had turned weakness into strength; they had won wars and defeated foreign armies. Women had welcomed loved ones who had died and come back to life. Others had been tortured and refused to yield and be released, hoping for a better resurrection.

Some were willingly abused and whipped, chained and imprisoned in dungeons, stoned, sawed in half, murdered and turned into cold corpses.

Others were wrapped in animal skins and left without homes, friends, or power. The world was no place for them! They walked on the edge of this harsh world, making their way as best they could (Hebrews 11:32-38).

Christians in the Early Church Martyred by Burning at the Stake (20-23)

They took the Christians to the armory and showed them the various weapons (swords, shields, helmets, armor, and shoes) that the master of the house had prepared to arm the pilgrims. They also showed them some of the tools that the Lord's workers had used to do amazing things. For example, Moses' staff (Exodus 17:9), the stake and club that Jael used to kill Sisera (Judges 4:21), the empty jar, trumpet, and torch that Gideon used to fight and defeat the Midianite army (Judges 7:16-23), and the sword with which the Lord will destroy sinners in His future judgment (Jeremiah 21:9).

It was the next morning. Christian was led to the top of the roof by the three virgins. As Christian looked to the south, he saw the Delectable Mountains spread out in the distance, very beautiful and pleasing to the eye.

Delectable Mountains (2020)

Lush forests, vineyards, orchards with all kinds of fruit trees, beautiful flowers of all colors, endless springs and fountains…it was a sight to behold, a sight that is hard to describe. The land was called the Land of Immanuel, and it was the next stop on Christian's journey.

Finally, Christian put on the full armor of God (James 6:11) and set out on his pilgrimage. His body was already equipped with the girdle of truth, the spectacles of righteousness, the gospel of peace, the shield of faith, the helmet of salvation, and the sword of the Spirit, and so he set out for the Delectable Mountains.

A Beautiful Home While Studying Abroad

If there was ever a beautiful house that stood out in his memory, it was the house in Germany where I stayed while studying abroad. Christian spent three days in that beautiful house, but I stayed there for six years. If Christian found "prudence," "piety," and "charity," I found Mrs. C. Behrendt, my friend Heiner Doersam, and Professor U. Schmidt.

Mrs. Behrendt, my friend Heiner, and Professor Schmidt (2019)

Mrs. Berend was a compassionate woman who took care of me like a parent so that I could be married in a German church. My friend Heiner was a pharmacy student from a devout Christian family whom I met in a German church. Heiner was also my teacher who taught me German. He helped me to find and meet professors at different universities because of my lack of German communication skills. Prof. Schmidt was my advisor, a wise man who helped me secure a scholarship from the German government so that I could focus on my research in peace.

If it were not for these people, I would not be a professor of science in Korea and have a Christian family. They were all devoted to the Lord without expecting anything in return from me.

By God's grace, I also found rest in a beautiful house in Germany, a stork village. There are quite a few Stork Villages in Europe besides Germany, and I have visited most of them in Germany and France. Especially the Stork Village in Ribeauville, Alsace, France, is one of the most beautiful places in the world.

And by "beautiful" I mean people and storks living together in harmony.

How does a stork with a wingspan of 2 meters live with people?

Most storks in Europe nest on the roofs of man-made buildings. Visitors can look up and see the storks breeding on the roofs. The storks don't seem to mind the attention. When you look through the window and see a mother holding, feeding and nursing her newborn, the phrase "the storks bite the child" comes to mind.

Stork Village in Ribeauville, Alsace, France (2010)

The dormitory I stayed in was run by the Evangelical Church, and it wasn't a purpose-built facility. It was a house that someone had lived in all their life and donated to the Evangelical Church. It was a great place for an international student with no money like me.

Every Wednesday night we had a service led by the dormitory pastor. It felt very different from the church in Korea, because in German Protestantism, communion is not missing from every service. At first I was not used to it, but as I got used to it, I realized that the weekly communion was a precious gift from God that made me spiritually strong.

The Flesh and Blood of the Lord

The apostle Paul says that everyone who is a Christian is an invited guest at the table of Christ (Romans 14:4). Eugene Peterson, author of The Message Bible, advises the Christian lifestyle: "When you sit down at the table, you're not filling your stomach, you're sharing the life of Jesus. (Romans 14:21, The Message).

When Jesus broke bread for His disciples, He said, "This is my body" (Matthew 26:26), and then He gave them a cup and said, "This is my blood, the blood of the covenant" (Matthew 26:28). He then said, "Do this in memory of me" (Luke 22:19) at every meal.

The Last Supper (2022)

The Bible testifies to the life of Jesus as follows.

> Who, though he was in the form of God, did not count equality with God a thing to be grasped, but emptied himself, taking the form of a servant, being made in the likeness of men, and being found in the form of a man, he humbled himself and became obedient to the point of death, even death on a cross (Phil 2:6-8).

This life of Jesus is embodied in the sacraments, so that the bread and cup are not just a sign of his desire or need.

The bread and cup are his body and blood, which have died in our place, so that we can encounter Jesus, who is fully present to us in the sacrament.

Jesus comes to our homes even now and says.

"Your table is not my last meal with my disciples in that distant land long ago".

At every meal I am reminded of the sacrament of the Lord's presence. The Apostle Paul testifies to this when he says

> For as often as you eat this bread and drink this cup, you proclaim the Lord's death until he comes" (1 Corinthians 11:26).

When Jesus ate his last meal with his disciples and went to take up his cross, he promised to give new life to this body born in sin. He is now bringing the body of sin, which is death, into the life of life, which is eternal and unending.

What does this outpouring of God's gift through Jesus Christ bring us? The answer is also given by Paul.

There is no comparison between the sin that brings death and this gift that brings abundant life, for the verdict for that sin was death, but the verdict for the many other sins that followed was a verdict of wonderful new life" (Message Bible, Romans 5:17).

The Bible teaches us that "a life without Christ is a life spent striving for sin all the days of our lives. The pension we eventually receive is death. But the gift that God gives is true life, eternal life (Romans 6:23).

For me who believe this, the life of the flesh is gone, and the life of eternal life from the precious flesh and blood of the Lord is here to stay. With this confession, I set out on my next pilgrimage.

CHAPTER 8

AVOLUON

Being born as a human being is often associated with experiencing a series of trials. People of faith are no exception, which is why many of us find our faith. Perhaps the reason for keeping faith in difficult situations is to receive blessings from the world. This is why we often hear the phrase "gibogsin-ang" (religion praying for blessings), but God loves us so much that He allows even the downs. You can see this in the story of a certain elderly deaconess, which I will introduce below. Even on this pilgrimage of walking with the stork, the blade of the avoluon was pointed at me.

Leaving his beautiful home, Christian was confronted by a great monster whose name was Avoluon, the Lion of the Abyss (Apollyon 9:11). Filled with fear, Christian didn't know whether to turn and run or to face him. As he did so, Apollyon cried out terribly.

"Do not be afraid, for you have come from the city of destruction, and I have watched you closely. I am king, lord, and master in the place from which you came, and you were one of my subjects. Answer me, why have you forsaken your king?

In response, Christian makes his point.

"It is true that I was born in a country ruled by you, but serving you was very hard work, and the wages you paid me could not buy me life, for the wages of sin is death (Romans 6:23). So after I became a saint, I looked for ways to change myself, as any discerning person would do".

And so their conversation continued at length.

"What king would easily lose his people? I will never lose you. Come back with me, and I will give you riches so great that the world cannot contain them.

"Don't be ridiculous, don't you always lure people like that!

"Are you not already a traitor, and how many times have you gone out of his way?

"Yes, but I know that my God is a God of mercy, and He has forgiven me.

"Ugh - I am an enemy of God, I hate God and I hate His people.

Avoluon (2022)

Christian boldly proclaimed in the face of the fierce Aboluon.

"Beware, you destroyer! Beware, this is God's way!."

Avoluon didn't stop, but shook Christian.

"Do you not know that the end of those who have traveled this road after your god is disastrous?."

Once again, Christian stood his ground.

"This is the way I have chosen. No matter what happens now, I will be in the Kingdom of Heaven long after you and your world are gone and forgotten.

Avoluon saw this as a good opportunity and lunged at Christian, shouting.

"Yes, then I will play with you to my heart's content from now on!

He knocks the sword out of Christian's hand with such force that it falls to the ground. "Now, don't move," Aboluon yells and pushes Christian to the ground.

"Now, don't move!"

Christian was almost at death's door, but at that moment God helped him, and he reached out his hand and stabbed the devil with all his might, crying out

> "Rejoice not over me, my adversary. I may fall, but I will rise again." (Micah 7:8)

The Death of the Daughter of a Elder Deaconess

I realize that it is not easy for well-believing saints to overcome this kind of temptation from the devil. In the church I attended, there was a faithful deaconess who had a daughter. She was a good believer in Jesus and served the Lord diligently as a member of the choir. One day, she was suddenly taken to be with the Lord in the collapse of the Sampung Department Store. The deaconess felt that she had lost everything, and she lost her mind. She left the church for a while, doubting the existence of the God she had believed in.

As a Christian, when I face a great trial like this, I think of the Old Testament book of Job. Job was a godly, upright, blameless man. But then a trial came upon him. He lost his flock and all his possessions, and his body was afflicted with a terrible disease. His house collapsed, killing all of his beloved children.

"I have believed in God so diligently until now, so why are you giving me these trials?"

This must have been Job's cry, and after a period of complete silence, God responds.

> "Who are you to question my wisdom with ignorant and vain words? Now gird up your loins, stand up like a blacksmith, and answer my question. Were you present when I laid the foundations of the earth, and do you know who designed it, and do you know who laid the line of measurement on it? (...) When the waters burst forth from the heart of the earth, and who shut the floodgates and imprisoned the sea, it was I who covered the sea with clouds and shrouded it in darkness. It is I who made the sea a barrier of gold, so that it could not pass over it; it is I who shut up the sea and made it a gate". (Job 38:2-10)

Job 38:2-10 (2022)

This passage shows that our bodies and possessions are completely under God's sovereignty. As a Christian, I believe I could find myself in the same situation as Job, only I'm out of the way of Aboluon's battle, and Aboluon is something I could face at any moment. If I were to go to heaven right now, there's something I would ask God.

"God, why did You take her daughter?"

Faced with this question, I am reminded of the words of 1 Corinthians.

For now I see dimly as in a mirror, but then I shall see face to face, face to face; now I know in part, but then I shall know fully, as the Lord knows me" (1 Corinthians 13:12).

The Sermon on the Mount and the story of vineyard

In Matthew 5, Jesus climbs a mountain and speaks of eight blessings.

> "You're blessed when you feel you've lost what's most precious to you. Only then can you be embraced by the one who is most dear to you (Mt 5:4, Message).

Jesus didn't come as an earthly teacher; He came as God and tells us these words. The deaconess who lost what was most precious to her must have lived with the hope of being embraced by the One who was most precious to her.

The world often tells us that we are blessed if we are rich or if we live a long life without sickness, but Jesus does not speak of the blessings of the world. Jesus teaches us what it's like to live in the world ruled by God, the kingdom of God.

He teaches us not to live as reflexes to sin and guilt, not to live as people more powerful than us tell us to live, not to live out of desperation by taking whatever comes our way, not to live for survival in cynicism and

Christians Listening to a Sermon and Reciting the Sermon on the Mount (2023)

malice, and not to live selfishly by making our ego our master. In other words, He trains us to live in faith and love, to live according to the reality inherent in the kingdom of God.

In the biblical record, Jesus often used parables to explain to crowds what the kingdom of heaven is like. A classic example is the parable of the master who hired labourers to work in his vineyard (Matthew 20:1-16).

The parable says: 'The kingdom of heaven is like a householder who hired labourers to work in his vineyard. But if you look at the story as it unfolds, it doesn't make sense.

The vineyard owner is described as paying the workers arbitrarily, not in proportion to the hours they worked.

When I first came across this story, I thought God was being very unfair, but after meeting an 85-year-old man who works for a missionary organisation that helps drug and alcohol addicts, I got a clearer understanding of what God is like.

This man was once called the Great Thief by our society, because he was not a simple thief, but only broke into the houses of famous rich people and stole their riches.

I asked him a cautious question.

"By any chance, sir, how long did you spend in prison?"

"Yes, I was in prison for 45 years."

I couldn't help but doubt my ears for a moment: 45 years is a long time, and this is not the prisoner I had only seen in the film The Shawshank Redemption, but the man who was standing right in front of me!

When I met him, my first impression was not that he was 86, but that he looked 68. Only his hair was white and he was a fine old man with a graceful appearance.

He told me this story.

"I was abandoned in an orphanage when I was four years old, and from then on I didn't learn anything, so I just thought of ways to get by by stealing."

"You were never assaulted or tortured during those long years in prison?"

"Of course I was tortured many times. I was also caught stealing and shot by the police, once in Korea and once in Japan, and the bullets went close to my face and past my shoulder, but that's why I'm still alive today."

"How did you come to believe in Jesus?"

"I met Jesus through reading the Bible and, as you can see, I'm now helping a pastor who works in a community for recovering drug and alcohol addicts."

As I looked at this man, I wondered how God could allow such a life for someone born into the same human race.

A life without parents and only prison since childhood!

If he hadn't been abandoned by his parents, this saint's life would never have been like this!

Later in life I discovered an amazing secret of heaven.

The moment I realised this truth, that the kingdom of heaven gives the same denarius to the labourer in the vineyard who comes late, I became even more in awe of God.

Storks and President

The difficult stork restoration reached its peak seven years after the restoration. It was the fourth successful artificial breeding in the world. Since then, the number of storks has increased. We finally reached the point where we had a population of 100 storks returning to the wild in Korea, almost 50 years after the last stork disappeared in 1971 in Eumseong, Chungcheongbuk-do.

At the time, neighboring Japan had already reintroduced its first stork, with the Crown Prince and Crown Princess attending the ceremony, and the United States had just had President Clinton personally declare the reintroduction of the endangered American bald eagle.

"Could the president of our country come to a stork reintroduction ceremony, 44 years after it became extinct?"

At the time, all my attention was focused on that one question. As if in response to this fervent wish, I received a welcome phone call. A professor of ornithology in Korea informed me that he had been invited to the Blue House to give a lecture on "Korea's Birds.

He had always had a personal relationship with the president's secretary, so I figured that opportunities like this didn't come along every day. I asked the professor to mention the imminent return of the Korean stork to the wild in his speech. I also asked him to personally deliver the invitation letter I had written to the president. However, the president did not attend the lecture. Normally, the president would have sat in the front row and listened to the lecture, but at that time the president was staying at the presidential residence. At that time, the president was having trouble with Chung Yun-hoe's "three doorknobs". In the end, the professor had no choice but to hand the invitation letter to the secretary general and leave the Blue House.

I felt like a man who had lost everything in the world, and I was in a state of loss. I had just succeeded in artificially breeding storks, which was so difficult, after only 10 years. As I was in a quagmire about how this project was going to unfold, I thought of John Bunyan's unfolding story.

I thought, "Why did they bring him in at this point?"

I thought and thought and thought. In fact, if the president had attended the stork reintroduction ceremony, I would have asked him to change the name of the Stork Restoration Research Center from a private corporation to a public one. In retrospect, if that had happened, I might have become a complacent person.

"Am I doing this for the glory of God?"
I asked myself, and when I finally stood before God again, wounded by Abolton and limping, the words of a Bible verse struck my soul.

> "Because of the greatness of the revelation, He gave me a thorn in my flesh, a messenger of Satan, to afflict me, lest I should become arrogant" (2 Corinthians 12:7).

Before God and His Word, I confess that I do not do anything in the world by myself. The moment I realized that I was doing my stork research for my own glory, I decided to lay it down.

The Woman and the Stork (2015)

Avoluon

Every time there is a change of president, I send a letter to the new president. It's almost an international norm that leaders take action to restore endangered species in their countries, because that's what all developed countries do.

This was no exception. But I doubted that this president would take care of it, so I wrote a letter to the first lady.

The storks were reintroduced to the wild in Yesan County, Chungcheongnam-do, and to keep the birds alive, residents have to pay the government to preserve their habitat. The first lady personally visited the stork village in Yesan and asked for help in passing the law. Of course, I had already petitioned the National Assembly.

About two weeks later, I received an official letter from Yesan County saying, "Why are you bothering our county by sending this to the First Lady?" It was so ridiculous that the county's feelings were expressed in an official letter instead of a personal letter. I immediately regretted sending the letter to the First Lady.

Once again, the leader of our country fails to restore the storks!

Time passed, and just over two years into the new president's term, martial law was declared, which of course failed, but it left a deep scar on the people and divided the country into those who were for impeaching the president and those who were against.

I was proud of Korea as a democratic country and that we could join the ranks of developed countries for a short period of time, but my heart sank when I realized that we were going back to the past.

The church I attend held a special week-long dawn prayer for the nation. In the midst of the prayer, the people were confronted with a demon named Aboluon, a messenger from the abyss. Aboluon was a monster among demons, so powerful that when the people called for him to leave the prayer, he refused to back down.

I remember seeing the current president and his wife when he was a candidate. The presidential couple didn't even look ordinary to the average person. The presidential candidate at that time appeared on television with the words "Chinese King" written on his palm. The wife, who was his running mate, was too young for her husband and was deeply involved in shamanism.

John Bunyan presents Avoluon in the scene where he dueled with Christian in the heavenly court. Only by putting on the full armor of God in a beautiful house could "Christian" stand up to Aboluon and defeat the devil.

In modern history, the Korean people went through the bitter and turbulent times of the Japanese occupation and the Korean War. During the military dictatorship, the people fought against the oppression of the rulers and achieved democratization and rapid economic development. However, when the people were on the verge of entering the developed world, emergency martial law was imposed on them, which was only seen in military dictatorships.

The rule of law requires the president to cooperate with the investigation if he has illegally declared a state of emergency, but instead he is rallying his supporters and claiming the state of emergency as a means of governance. These supporters are even defending the president and putting pressure on the judges of the Constitutional Court, the last bastion of democracy.

The Lord tells Christians to pray: 'Lead us not into temptation, but deliver us from evil. I pause in my current pilgrimage to pray fervently for deliverance from Aboluon, the king of the devil. This prayer echoes loudly at dawn, and I am confident that the Lord will answer it.

The Bible presents David as the humblest of kings: he was a king, but he was a man who served God alone, a man who humbled himself before God, a man who was worthy in God's sight, a man most respected by his people, a national hero.

Jesus comes among us and teaches us humility, humbling himself to be a servant (John 13:1-16) and even being ashamed to die on a cross (Philippians 2:8).

A There is no humility in this Avoluon.

There is only destruction in him.

Today, on this pilgrimage, I pray to the Lord with my life, asking Him to defeat this Avoluon.

The Suspicious Couple (2022)

CHAPTER 9
THE VALLEY OF SHADOWS

Am I on the right pilgrimage?
As we walk through the "valley of the shadow of death"
(Psalm 23:4), questions like these can cause us to feel fear,
doubt, and panic. I've been tempted by sexual temptation,
and I've felt betrayed by people I trusted, but I know I'm
not alone on this journey, and I walk with the assurance
that God is with me until I reach the city of Zion.

As Christian entered the valley of the shadow of death, he heard the voice of the blind.

"This way~ come this way~ I know where you're going~ this way~"

"Ugh~"

The voices of the ghosts could be heard from inside the valley.

"Where the hell do you think you're going?"

"Do you know what you're doing?"

"God doesn't even know you?"

"God doesn't even know you're here!"

"You will die if you continue!"

"You'll fall from there!"

"Don't you want to go back, don't you want to run away?"

"You will die!"

Christian repeated in a subsonic voice.

"No, this is not the voice of my heart.

"God, be with me, give me strength!"

The voice of the one who had gone before was heard.

"Yea, though I walk through the valley of the shadow of death, I will fear no evil: for thou art with me. (Psalm 23:4)

When Christian heard this, the fear of the valley of the shadow of death finally left him and he saw a man walking in the distance. He quickened his pace and spoke to him. It was Faithful, who was from the same area as Christian. Christian greeted him happily.

"Dear brother Faithful, I am very happy to have caught up with you and met you. I thank God for melting our hearts so that we could travel together like this.

The Grim Valley of Death (2022)

Faithful answered as if he had been waiting.

"My dear friend, I had planned to come with you when we left the city where we lived, but you left first and I was forced to travel this long way alone."

Christian confessed his journey to his disciple.

Then, as if he'd been waiting for it, Faithful spoke up, and their conversation continued.

"Fortunately, I did not fall in, and I made it safely to the wicket gate, but on the way I met a wicked woman named 'Lust,' and it could have been disastrous. She lured me into her chamber and persisted in offering me all sorts of pleasures and delights."

"I don't suppose you would have complied with her wishes?"

"Of course I didn't defile myself, but I was reminded of a verse from a book I read some time ago: 'Her steps go forth like a stallion' (Prov. 5:5). So I closed my eyes so I wouldn't be tempted by her dazzling appearance. Then she left, cursing all sorts of things, and I continued on my way.

The Wanton

This is not a unique experience for Faithful. I also remember acting on my sexuality. I was in college, at a time in my life when I had a very high sex drive.

I was hanging out with some friends, and we went to an ellow house with what was called a public brothel, where a man would pick a woman of his choice, be escorted to a bedroom, and sleep with her. I couldn't sleep all night with the whore next to me.

I remembered the story of Joseph who had to resist the constant temptations of Potiphar's wife and sneak out of her room (Genesis 39:9-12). He made it out alone at 4 a.m. when the curfew was lifted. For a Christian to pay for sex, I thought, was a violation of God's command in the seventh commandment, "Thou shalt not commit adultery" (Exodus 20:14).

The Bible says that "simply lusting after a woman is adultery." Since then, I have deeply repented to God for being drawn to the brothel and lusting after it, and I have decided never to live in such lust again.

The Wanton (2014)

Walking with the stork in the valley of the shadow of death

I didn't know that the "valley of the shadow of death" (Psalm 23:4) awaited me on my pilgrimage. Having just retired from my job, I rented a room in a town in Yesan County. I paid for the room with my retirement money. Since my home was in Seoul, I only went to Seoul on weekends, and on Mondays I would take the train from Shingil Station to Cheonan. Of course, I took the train from Cheonan to Yesan, which was easy because there was a free ride for senior citizens from Shingil Station to Cheonan, which is connected to the subway. On the other hand, I had to pay extra for transportation from Cheonan to Yesan because it was a national railway, but I had no choice. So for two years, I repeated the journey back and forth between Seoul and Yesan, rain or shine.

In the room I was given, I didn't have to do anything special; all I did all day was draw watercolors on hanji (traditional Korean) paper. The only time I went out was to visit the village where I wanted to restore the storks, which was Daesul-myeon, Yesan-gun, where there was an elderly man named Kim Jung-cheol who was the stork keeper.

I was the director of the Stork Ecology Research Center at Korea National University of Education (KNUE), and I was in charge of restoring the storks at Yesan Stork Park in Chungcheongnam-do. Just before I left KNUE, I sent a request to the president for the position of special researcher at the Stork Ecology Research Center, and I rented a room with an allowance to pay the rent. However, the president did not accept my position as a special researcher because he only listened to the successor director.

I had to cut all ties with the storks I had been breeding since that day. After I retired, I had more work to do to restore the storks, but God would not allow me to do it anymore. There was nothing more I could do for the storks and the people in the village where they lived except to pray to God every day.

I walked and walked and walked, hoping that my prayers would bring me through the valley of the shadow of death, thinking that I shouldn't stop my pilgrimage.

Prayer at the Place of a Single Vase (2018)

The Talkative

While you were talking to Faithful, a "Talkative" walked down the street. He spoke to Talkative, and their conversation began

"Friend, where are you going, are you on your way to heaven?"

"Yes, I am on my way there, and I will gladly accompany you if you wish."

"Then let us walk together and pass the time talking of good and right things.

"I like to talk about good and right things, and I really like to talk about religion and the Bible and God."

"It is so meaningful to talk about these things."

"That's exactly what I meant."

At this point, Christian says something to Faithful that is attributed to him. On behalf of Christian, Faithful asked Talkative again.

"Mr. Talkative, can you tell me how the grace of God has changed your life?"

"First it taught me to say that sin is bad."

"Isn't grace what makes you despise and hate sin?"

"That's what I said, I'm always shouting that sin is bad. Well, anybody can shout from the pulpit that sin is bad and take it home and live with it. I also have a great knowledge of religion and the Bible."

Faithful had some sharp advice for talkers with a pretentious religious outlook.

"A person can know everything in the Bible and not believe it, just as a servant can know his master's will and not obey it. You can have all the knowledge in the world and not have wisdom. Wisdom is a gift from God."

But Talkative was interrupted and stormed off.

"Now, you two," said Christian, "you are very determined to get the capsule. You and I have different ideas, so I'll just go my own way."

Christians and believers have come to think of Talkative as someone who loudly condemns sin but inwardly accepts it without

Faithful, Christian, and Talkative (2022)

reservation. When grace works in the heart, the evidence is obvious, and Talkative was someone who could talk easily but had never experienced saving grace working in the heart.

I think it's a blessing from God that we meet people well on this pilgrimage, but sometimes we don't, and we fall into the "valley of the shadow of death. It was a blessing that Christian met Faithful, but it was a great woe that I met Talkative.

Talkative who sold the storks

I reached retirement age without finishing my stork restoration work. I tried very hard to train a successor, but it didn't work out. The university didn't choose the person I had trained. The only person I trusted to take over was a professor of environmental studies. She took over the stork restoration work I had been doing for 20 years and turned it into her own business. I knew her to be a Christian, but she was a total talker when it came to stork restoration.

When I was at the university, there was a "stork policy" which stated that the president of the university owned the storks I raised. Talkative, who was the successor to the Stork Ecology Research Center, sold the property to the Cultural Heritage Administration, which is in charge of Korea's natural monuments, and built the Stork Ecology Research Center building on the university campus. Of course, it was not ostensibly sold for money, but it was done secretly on the condition that the president of the university would not claim ownership of the storks. Thus, the restoration of Korea's storks was no longer the work of a naturalist, but in the hands of an administrator and a gossip obsessed with fame.

After that, the Talkative received the Presidential Award from the Cultural Heritage Administration and the Environmental Award from the Ministry of Environment for successfully restoring the Korean storks. In a way, the Talkative was a person who looked good on the outside, but had no inside, and used the storks only to show off his sense of honor.

I'm reminded of the words of an ornithologist.

"The success of stork restoration is something only God can do."

If this is true, then stork restoration is a project that brings glory to God, the Sovereign of Creation, because if it succeeds, if it wins a prize, it belongs to the people. Why the people?

Storks are birds that live where people live. It is necessary for people to stop spraying pesticides for the storks, and it is also necessary for people to create a biodiverse rice field environment for the storks. For these reasons, it is unlikely that successful stork restoration will happen in Korea in the near future.

Should we look forward to it in 50 or 100 years?

So the Talkavtive went around bragging that the restoration of storks in our country was a success, and even built a building and received an award. This caused me, as a scientist, to have a mental breakdown. Because there was nothing I could do about it proactively.

Judas Iscariot was paid 30 pieces of silver to hand Jesus over to the authorities, and Jesus already knew this. Jesus had not resisted since the kiss of Judas Iscariot.

After years of teaching, preaching, healing, and doing whatever He wanted, He was now completely in the hands of the enemy. In the end,

The Kiss of Judas Iscariot (2021)

this Judas was just an instrument of God's work. I confess today that this Judas is not irrelevant to me, and it is more important to realize that.

Like everyone else, most of my life is determined by things that happen to me from the outside, things over which I have no control. There is only a small part of my life that is determined by my active behavior. I have been conditioned to want everything to be an action that starts with me. I have even hated when others have betrayed me, but the Lord wants me to let go of even that.

I realize that so much of my life is passive, not active, and I confess that I need a life focused solely on the Lord, a pilgrimage that leads to such a life.

CHAPTER 10
THE MARKETPLACE OF VANITIES

We live in a time of materialism and overconsumption. It is indeed difficult to keep the faith in this age, but there has been a "faithfulness." Just as Jesus met the Samaritan woman in the "marketplace of vanities," He gave eternal life to my sister and made her a child in whom God was well pleased.

After the journey through the wilderness, Christian and Faithful came to the marketplace of vanities, which is the place you have to go through to get to heaven. It was the only way to get to heaven, and if you didn't go through it, you were out of the world.

About 5,000 years ago, pilgrims were just as honest and pious as they are today. When Beelzebub and Avoluon realized that pilgrims had to pass through the City of Vanities, they and their allies conspired to set up a marketplace inside the City of Vanities where they could buy and sell all kinds of vanities.

In this marketplace, all kinds of earthly things were for sale: houses, lands, places of honor, commercial goods, titles, honors, nations, kingdoms, lusts, pleasures, and so on. For pleasure there were prostitutes, wives, husbands, children, masters, servants, life, blood, flesh, souls, silver, gold, pearls, and other precious stones. In addition, there were shamans, charlatans, gamblers, ruffians, and all sorts of other lovers of pleasure and vices. Even Jesus himself was tempted by Beelzebub as he passed through these streets 2,000 years ago. Had he submitted to Beelzebub, he would have made him lord of the streets of vanity.

As Christian and Faithful entered the marketplace of vanities, they heard cries everywhere.

"Buy stuff, buy stuff, buy stuff!"

"Collect stuff, take care of stuff, start a new life!"

"Keep your stuff shiny and well-kept, and everyone will want your stuff, and you'll be important!"

"Be famous! Everyone will want to be like you!"

"Don't you want to be more beautiful than everyone else? I'll make you that way. If you're prettier, you're a better person."

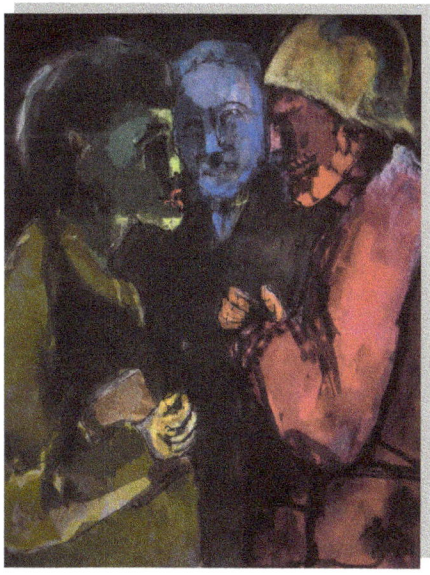

Faithful Arguing with a Market Seller (2022)

A merchant approached them and asked.

"What on earth are you looking for?"

"We are looking for the truth.

The merchant, who witnessed this, became suspicious of the two pilgrims and reported them to the market owner. Caught by the market owner, Christian and Faithful were taken to court for disturbing the order of the market.

The Court of Vanity (2015)

"I am a 'good-hating' judge. You have been accused of several crimes. You have caused much controversy and influenced some with your dangerous ideas, and we cannot tolerate that. As much as we hate to admit it, the people of the Marketplace of Vanities could easily leave here. If they think there's something better out there. And by not participating in the market, you become criminals. Furthermore, your dangerous ideas might cause others to leave the market as well, so you are our enemies. Sentence. Lock you in the dungeon and beat you until you change your mind about joining our market order!

As the judge finished his sentence, there was chatter in the courtroom.

"I, two people went through the market yesterday, they said they didn't buy anything..."

"Honor, glory, money, land, crowns, jewels, all these things I would gladly give them, but they passed by as if they were nothing..."

"Others say that seeing them like this might make us rethink the value of our things.

"You've caused so much controversy in the marketplace!"

It was also very loud outside the courtroom.

"What the hell did they do to deserve to be put in the dungeon?"

"They broke the peace! They brought chaos to the marketplace!"

"How so, they were just passing through, they didn't say anything bad to anyone..."

"That's not the point, their wrong ideas are leading people down strange paths!"

"I don't get it, if people want to leave the market and follow them, they should be able to!"

"Dude, I can't talk to you anymore."

"There's a lot of chaos in the market, and we have to do something about it!"

This outcry brought the trial back to court, and the judge laid down the law.

"Bring in one of them and make an example of him! He shall be beheaded immediately. If there is still confusion, I will make an example of the other.

Thus, on a snowy day, Faithful was hanged from a tree on a mountain slope to die a horrible death.

Martyrdom of the Pilgrims (2019)

The Stork in Court

One day, the country took me to court on behalf of this stork. The charge was "unauthorized use of state land". I built a stork aviary on government land without informing the government. I was charged with 100 million won in compensation for unauthorized use of government land.

Stork restoration in Korea began in 1971 in Eumseong, Chungcheongbuk-do, after the last wild stork was shot by a wheat harvester. Since there were no storks left in the wild, it was necessary to introduce storks from Russia. An aviary was built in a corner of the campus of the national university where I worked, and the birds were bred in captivity. At first no one was interested.

Over time, as the number of storks grew and the day of their release into the wild approached, the university's provost began looking into the ownership of the storks, starting with a lawsuit for eminent domain and demanding the dissolution of the Center for Stork Restoration and Research, the organization that had bred and operated the storks. When I took my hands off, there were people who wanted to do things with the greedy mindset of getting something out of the storks. They saw me as a competitor with bad motives, and they think that the worse my situation gets, the better their situation will be.

How should I respond?

Whether their motives are pure, evil, or unclear, I choose not to care. I choose to trust God and leave everything in His hands.

When storks lived in the country

Rural South Korea was very poor, and people began to flock to the cities to escape their poor rural lives. It was probably around this time that the country's top policy shifted to improving the countryside to increase crop yields and improve the lives of poor Koreans.

To reduce labor, agriculture was mechanized, farmland was cleared and heavily sprayed with herbicides and pesticides. Our eating culture also changed to a meat-based diet, and many livestock farms were built on rural farmland. The runoff and manure from these farms began to degrade stork habitat.

My family left the countryside at an early age, and my father and mother were involved in trade. I had an older sister who was eight years older than me. My sister carried me around and raised me instead of my parents, who were busy with their business. In those days, the first-born daughter was the breadwinner. There wasn't enough money for her to go to college. When she graduated from high school, she was expected to get married.

As marriage approached, my sister was rotting her parents' insides. When her father found out, he beat her to death, but when she left the house, he caught her and cut off all her hair with scissors. Her hair looked like it had been eaten by rats. It was late in life that she accepted the Lord as her personal Savior.

She died in a nursing home. I wasn't there on her deathbed, but I was told the brief words she spoke before she died.

"Jesus, receive my soul!"

A Girl Carrying a Newborn Baby (2016)

When she was still alive, I, the eldest son, had to take care of my mother, and my sister arranged a single room for her. All I could do was to give her a small allowance from my professor's salary. She called me "Professor!"

That's what she called me. She was very proud of her brother, whom she raised because he was once known on television and in the newspapers as a professor who restored Korean storks.

She took care of my mother for more than 20 years, even when she was diagnosed with brain cancer. She never showed signs of struggle, and she never lived a worldly life; rather, she lived a joyful life, always grateful to the Lord. The secret of her faithfulness to the Lord can only be explained by a personal encounter with Jesus.

There is a scene in the Bible where a Samaritan woman meets Jesus. Jesus asks her for a drink of water when she comes out to draw water. This is the beginning of the conversation between Jesus and the Samaritan woman. In the Bible, the conversation is recorded as follows.

> "You are a Jew, how can you ask me, a Samaritan woman,
> for a drink of water?" (John 4:9)

If you knew God's generosity and who I am, you would have asked me for a drink and I would have given you living water" (John 4:10).

Jesus was already aware of this Samaritan woman's promiscuity with men, which led her to intuit that Jesus was the Savior. Jesus then said.

> "Everyone who drinks of this water will be thirsty again.
> But whoever drinks the water I will give him will never
> thirst again. The water I will give him will become in him
> a well of water springing up to eternal life (John 4:14).

The Samaritan Woman (2022)

The elder sister has already returned to the eternal kingdom, not thirsting for the water of the world, but drinking living water from the fountain of life given by the Lord.

As I look at the faithfulness of the Heavenly Father, I see an overlap with the preaching and life of Deacon Stephen, whose sermon adorns Acts 7:1-53. He boldly defended the Gospel before the Council and was stoned to death by an unruly congregation who heard his sermon. Just before he was stoned, he cried out.

"Jesus! Receive my spirit" (Acts 7:59).

The Christian life is eternal and unending, which is why the last cry of Deacon Stephen as he enters into new life is so fully conveyed. The Apostle Paul, watching this scene from the sidelines, confessed after his conversion.

"As though we were unknown, yet we are known; as though we were dead, yet behold, we are alive; as though we were chastened, yet we were not killed; as though we were troubled, yet we rejoice always; as though we were poor, yet we enrich many; as though we had nothing, yet we have everything (2 Corinthians 6:9-10).

Do I now have the faith to please the Lord like my elder sister?

Though all the storks are gone, I am leaving this market of vanities, hoping that a repentance like Paul's will be my prayer.

CHAPTER 11

MR. GRIPE-MAN

Today's society has become one where you have to be born into a golden family to get ahead and be treated well. Not only that, but you have to have superior genes to be appreciated. John Bunyan speaks through the mouths of people from the "city of accumulation" and denounces the spirit of the age. He is referring to the phenomenon of a society where the pastor is paid a large salary because he is good at preaching and the congregation grows.
On this pilgrimage with the storks, I was able to meet the disciples of "Mr. Gripe-Man" who live in our society today. It is difficult to even use the term 'only faith' in this society.

After leaving the "city of vanity," Christian went on a pilgrimage with Hopefull. Along the way, the two pilgrims met Mr. Hold-World, Mr. Money-Love, and Mr. Save-All. They were the disciples of a teacher in the City of Greed who taught them violence, deceit, flattery, lies, and all the other tricks that make faith a sham.

Mr. Hold-World, Mr. Money-Love, and Mr. Save-all from the City of Mr. Gripe-man (2021)

Christian overheard a conversation between Mr. Hold-World, Mr. Money-Love, and Mr. Save-all.

Mr. Hold-World: "Who are those people in front of us? They seem to be on the same pilgrimage as us, so why aren't they looking down on us?

Mr. Money-Love: "We have read that people who are too righteous are too high-minded, and when they judge people, they use their arguments to condemn and judge those who are not like them.

Mr. Save-all: I believe in God too, and since God has given us so much in this world, doesn't it make sense to honor Him by being good stewards of what He has given us?

Mr. Hold-World: "I think we all agree on that point.

Mr. Money-Love: "I think it is right for pastors to be well paid and to work for the saints. If the pastor's sermons are good, he collects a lot of money from the congregation and builds a big chapel out of it, isn't that glorifying to God?"

Eventually, Christian was forced to interrupt them and share his thoughts.

"A person of faith, even a child, can answer a thousand such questions: It is unlawful for a man to follow Jesus even for the sake of bread. How abominable it is to use Jesus and religion to gain temporal pleasures and advantages! You will find such behavior only among unbelievers and hypocrites, devils and witches. When Hamor and Shechem coveted Jacob's daughters and cattle in the days of old, but found that they could have access to them only if they were circumcised like the Jews, they said, "If we also circumcise all our men, as they were all circumcised, shall not their cattle, their beasts, their possessions, and everything else be ours? In other words, they sought to use religion as a means to achieve their goal of obtaining Jacob's daughters and livestock."

Spiritual Treasure in a Clay Pot

Sometimes, I could find no trace of Jesus in the perching of certain pastors, which made me question their spiritual guidance. I call this the 'trace of Jesus', which stems from the discrepancy between the content of their sermons and how they live their lives. As a pilgrim, I felt great disappointment when I encountered pastors like Mr. Money-Love from the city of accumulation. Today's pastors have become a profession in society, and the message they preach differs greatly from that of the apostles in the early Church.

In 2 Corinthians (4:5), the Apostle Paul wrote to the church in Corinth, 'We do not preach ourselves, but Jesus Christ as Lord.' He also says that God has shone in their hearts to give them the light of the knowledge of the glory of God in the face of Jesus Christ. Paul calls this 'treasure'. He likens this 'treasure' to a vessel within our bodies, describing it as both a ' spiritual treasure' and a 'tremendous power' from God.

While I can respect the role of pastor, I disagree with Mr Money-Love's idea that 'if a pastor's preaching is good, it is glorifying to God to collect large offerings from the congregation and use them to build a large church'.

According to Paul's message in 2 Corinthians 4:10, 'every Christian carries the death of Jesus in their body so that the life of Jesus may also be manifested in their body'. This verse helped me discover the biblical truth that the life of Jesus should be manifested in a Christian's body, and that eventually the death of a Christian will be swallowed up by the life of Jesus.

The Descendants of Mr. Gripe-Man

One day I realized that the stork restoration project was not a research project of a natural scientist, but a sacrifice of "Mr. Hold-World," "Mr. Money-Love," and "Mr. Save-all" from the city of Mr. Grip-Man.

A media company is quite famous in Korea. What made me think of the media company as Mr Hold-World, Mr Money-Love and Mr Save-all from the city of accumulation was that it worked on the side of the corrupt and powerful rather than reporting fairly for the public. It is also well known that it is paid by chaebol (tycoons) to report in the interests of those chaebol-companies.

This media company has been urging me to apply for environmental awards through its reporter for decades, and finally organised a prize fund and awarded it to the head of a local government organisation that indiscriminately released storks into the wild, under the name of the 'Korea-Japan International Environmental Award'.

It wasn't a lot of money, but it was heartbreaking to realize that releasing storks into the wild is a research project, and that the true nature of the project is being masked by packaging it as environmental protection.

"My country's stork restoration project has been thoroughly exploited by the people of Mr. Grip-Man's City!"

As much as my heart broke, the storks must have been heartbroken too, because bad things happened to them after that.

Some of the storks I released died from being electrocuted by utility poles, and others suffered from pesticide poisoning.

One day I saw a picture of a stork on a website I run, and I was horrified: it was walking around with one of its legs tangled in a fishing line, and one of its legs had been cut off.

If the rich, the obsessed, and the old, if they have money and shout the glory of God, why shouldn't they contribute money to put the telephone poles underground? Of course, I know it's almost impossible for them because they have been taught by their ancestors to use violence, fraud, flattery, lies, and all sorts of tricks to get their way.

Unbeknownst to me, a poster was put up at the school where I was working saying that "Professor Park was using land for his personal research that was meant for public use by school members," and demanding that he leave the school immediately. After 10 years at the university, I was faced with being kicked out of the university because of my research on stork restoration. I temporarily stopped my research on campus and went to Insa-Dong Seoul. The idea was to introduce the stork to a large number of people.

In Insa-Dong, Professor Hoseop Yoon, who teaches environmental design at Kookmin University, was already doing environmental work. With Professor Yoon's permission, I handed out the stork mobile and the brochures I had prepared next to him. That day, I had something I wanted people to know.

The last storks in Korea were shot by poachers and have completely disappeared, and we need to regenerate our polluted nature to bring them back to the wild.

The response was so enthusiastic that Prof. Yoon drew T-shirts for a hundred passersby every day.

A few years later, when COVID-19 hit, I went to Insa-dong and Yeouido Ecological Circulation Road with my own paints and brushes. I organized Demonstration No. 1 in front of the National Assembly to petition the National Assembly that if farmers farmed without using pesticides, the government should support the reduction of emissions as an ecological management fee.

Drawing a picture in Insa-Dong (2004)

This is why the "Stork Law" is also known as the "Basic Law on the Ecological Management of Agricultural Land". This is because the storks, which depend on the rice fields, which are the private property of the residents, can only survive if the residents do not use pesticides. Ultimately, the petition failed because it did not meet the requirement of at least 50,000 signatures to be considered by a parliamentary subcommittee.

All attempts were unsuccessful and there was nothing I could do to restore the storks.

I had to leave the storks in God's hands, and praying was all I could do.

One day I had a dream.

An angel appeared, placed an old man in front of me, showed me a big white paper and said something to me. I still don't know what those words meant. But I do know that when my daughter's baby is born and becomes a girl, there will come a time when she will stand in front of the Capitol and ask the question.

"Do you know my grandfather?"

Someone will answer that question.

Do you know my grandfather? (2022)

"He stood in front of the Capitol every day to make the Stork Law."

In my dream I was still working for the storks.

You can't buy a stork back into the wild; you can only hope that one day, if we all change our minds and hearts, it will happen. The Lord is with me in my failures. This is what the Bible says about failure.

Even when our work seems to end in failure, inwardly God is extending grace and creating new life day by day. The hard times of the present pale in comparison to the blessed times to come, the great feast prepared for us. For what we see is not everything: what we see is here today and will be gone tomorrow, but what is invisible will last forever" (2 Corinthians 4:16-18, The Message).

Childlike minds

If I were a Nobel Prize-winning scientist, people wouldn't treat me like this. And my research on stork restoration wouldn't have ended in such a failure!

Whenever I experience failure as a Christian, it's easy to attribute it to a "lack of virtue on my part." But for me, the stork restoration worker, the Bible says this.

Do not compare yourself with others out of envy or pride. Do not strive to be what you are not" (Romans 12:6. The Message).

According to these words, it is a sin to judge others out of envy or pride, and to "strive to be what you are not" is to deny who God made you to be. Respect for others is important. However, as a scientist and a Christian, I felt that I was not living a Holy Spirit-led life. One day I learned a lesson from the Bible.

> Whoever receives one such little child in my name receives me; and whoever receives me does not receive me, but the one who sent me" (Mark 9:37).

When Jesus was home, he asked his disciples.
"What were you discussing on the road?"
The disciples had been arguing among themselves about who was the greatest. When they were silent, Jesus said to them, "If you want to be first, go to the end.

> "If you want to be first, go to the last place. Be the servant of all" (Luke 9:35).

Having said this, he placed a child in the middle of the room, took him in his arms and said to him

> "Whoever embraces one of these little ones, as I do, embraces me, and more than me, he embraces the God who sent me" (Mk 9:37).

What does it mean to receive or embrace a child?

We read in the Lord's teaching: "Give loving attention to those who are often ignored.

One day I met a beggar on the street who asked me for change, saying he was trying to buy something to eat. I didn't expect much of a reaction, but when I gave him a ten-thousand-won piece, he jumped up and said.

"Thank you."

He was surprised to receive such a large amount of money, but my heart was suddenly overwhelmed with sadness. In fact, he was on his way to a meeting that day that he didn't want to miss, and he didn't want to stop going to the meeting. So he didn't greet the beggar; he was just trying to be a good person.

This kind of kindness is very different from the Lord's words, "Take a little child" (Mark 9:37). All this time I have been expecting others to change their hearts, while failing to change mine.

Jesus Receives Little Children (2022)

Jesus addresses the disciples' competitive spirit by holding a child. As I watched this scene, I thought to myself, why would the Lord use the receiving of a child when He was pointing out the worldly competitiveness of the disciples?

There is a man who collects dirty garbage in the early morning hours, and among the garbage is the disposable diaper of a child that he has just thrown away. The mother of the little child says to him.

"Oh, sweetie, aren't you so grateful to the old man who just picked up the diaper you pooped in! It's because of him that you're healthy and not sick."

But the other mother said

> "Honey, if you don't study, you'll be a garbage collector like him. Do you really want to be a garbage collector with dirty clothes like that?"

The disciples' competitive spirit is their mother's idea, and Jesus asks the pilgrims from the city of "Mr. Grip-man" who will always be greater in the kingdom. I may be a failure on earth in my stork restoration research, but I hope I won't be a failure in heaven. So let's get rid of this idea of attributing failure to my lack of virtue.

"I'm a scientist, not a Nobel Prize winner!"

We're always comparing, as if someone is better and someone is not good enough. But a child doesn't judge and compare in that way. That's why Jesus said to take in a little child, because a child has a heart that doesn't judge.

CHAPTER 12
THE PRISON OF DESPAIR

*Just because you are a Christian doesn't mean you
don't feel pain that makes you want to die.
"Let me take my own life!"
It's not that the thought hasn't crossed our minds; the Lord
calls it "murder." Rather, He says to pray as if you were
ready to die, and He will answer you. In The Heavenly
Path, John Bunyan says this about prayer.
"The Lord has given to all believing saints that mysterious
key which opens the door of the castle prison of doubt."*

Christian and Hopeful take what appears to be an easy path, but soon find themselves in a pit. After struggling to climb out of the pit, Christian and Hopeful find a hut and fall asleep, exhausted and worn out. They are captured by the Giant of Despair and imprisoned in the dungeon known as Castle of Doubt.

Castle of Doubt Dungeon (2022)

As they entered the dungeon, the Giant of Despair shouted.

"Where have you come from, and how dare you enter my land?"

The Christians quickly replied.

"We are pilgrims, and we have lost our way."

The giant dragged them away and locked them in a dungeon, where they spent days without a sip of water or a crumb of bread.

The Giant of Despair had a wife, and her name was Suspicion. When the giant asked Suspicion what he should do with these two, she gave him this advice.

"Beat them to death until they take their own lives."

Christian, who was suffering in the dungeon, turned to Hopeful and said.

"Brother, what should we do? The life we're living is miserable, and I don't know if we should go on like this or take our own lives. I would rather suffocate and die than suffer this bone-crushing pain in my heart. A grave would be more comfortable than this dungeon."

Hopeful replied.

"I would rather die than live with such pain," he said, "but let us think about it. The Lord of the Kingdom of Heaven, where we are going, has commanded, 'Thou shalt not kill.' Suicide is also murder, so of course there is no eternal life."

In their anguish, the two began to pray, a prayer that lasted almost until daylight. It was just before dawn. Christian looked half-stunned and suddenly began to rage.

My daughter is a born-again Christian. I thought she was a good and smart girl, but as an adult she often got drunk at dinner parties and lost her mind. She also developed sleepwalking symptoms where she would wander the streets alone at night and never find her way home. On such occasions, we call them "movie breaks." On those days, I couldn't even communicate with her on my cell phone. It was unbearable as a parent. I was so scared because I didn't know when it would lead to an accidental death. As a woman, the thought that someone might molest her also drove me crazy as a father. I thought it was the devil's evil coming from my father, so it was better for me to die. I decided to die, so I began to fast and pray. On the sixth day of fasting, I wrestled with the devil. I commanded the demon to leave me in the name of Jesus.

The Desperate Giant and Suspicion (2022)

"Your faith has saved you" (Mark 10:52).

Holding on to these words, I prayed to be born again as an heir of the kingdom. Then, in a vision, God showed me the walls of my daughter's living room decorated with colorful pastel flowers. This opened the door to the castle prison of doubt.

Over the next six months or so, the demon that had been tormenting my daughter for years was gone and she was completely delivered from a life of captivity to the demon of alcohol to the point where she couldn't even drink a drop of alcohol. I praise God that He is alive and working now.

I was very worried about my daughter and I sent her to a psychiatrist for alcohol treatment in a general hospital but to no avail. When modern medicine failed to cure her, I clung to the Lord in prayer, ready to die, and a miracle happened that opened the door to my despair.

The Miraculous Prayer

As Christians, we too can be trapped in the prison of despair in our lives, and the only way out is through prayer. Peter, who was in prison and praying fervently, had a miracle happen: the doors were opened (Ac 12:1-10).

Being imprisoned in a prison of despair is a situation that can happen to any Christian or hopeful person, including you and me. Praying in this despair is not easy. Praying fervently, especially life-changing prayer, is even harder. But when Peter and other early church Christians prayed fervently enough to lay down their lives, the Lord answered with the miracle of an open door.

Why would John Bunyan think of a prison of despair?

As he pondered this thought, the miraculous moment of Peter's imprisonment unfolded before his eyes: the sudden opening of the prison gates.

At that very moment, the idea of executing some members of the church had entered King Herod's mind. He had killed James, the brother of John, and, realizing that this had increased his popularity among the Jews, he had Peter arrested and imprisoned, this time with four groups of four false soldiers guarding him. Herod planned to publicly execute Peter after Passover. While Peter was under heavy guard in prison, the church prayed more fervently for him.

The story that follows these words is truly dramatic. The time had finally come for Herod to take him out and execute him. That night, Peter was praying in his chains when suddenly an angel appeared at his side. In an instant, the prison was filled with light. The angel shook Peter and awakened him.

"Hurry!"

A Woman's Drunkenness (2022)

At that moment, the chains were removed from Peter's wrists and he did as the angel told him and stepped through the open gates into the street. This incredible moment of wonder came to me as a painting.

When Christian and Hopeful were first imprisoned in the prison of despair, they had forgotten to pray. But around midnight they began to pray, and they continued to pray until almost dawn. At sunrise, Christian suddenly thought of a solution and finally confessed

"What a fool I am to be stuck in this stinking cell when I could have gotten out any time I wanted, and I've forgotten the key to the covenant that I keep close to my heart and with which I can open any door in the castle of doubt.

This is a confession that is all too familiar to me, even as I walk with the stork. For God assures me that He will answer my prayers if I pray earnestly.

> "You shall call to me, and I will answer you, and I will show you great and secret things that you do not know" (Jer. 33:3).

Holding on to these words, I'll continue the rest of my pilgrimage in the fear of God."

Peter in Prison (2023)

CHAPTER 13

THE DELECTABLE MOUNTAIN

Today I am going to climb the Delectable Mountain and meet the God of power. John Bunyan shows us the last of the apostates through the shepherds, and we discover the secret of direct communication with the hitherto inaccessible God of omniscience.

Christian and Hopeful arrived at Mount Delectable, where the shepherds, the owners of the mountain, welcomed them and explained the mountain to them.

"This mountain belongs to Immanuel, in view of his city, and the sheep also belong to him, because he gave his life for them."

Christian first asked one of the shepherds.

"Is this the way to the City of Heaven?"

"You are on the right road."

"How far is the city of heaven?"

"Some people can't go very far, but everyone who is supposed to go there does."

The shepherds took the two pilgrims to the top of a mountain called "Error," which looked very steep. When they looked down, they saw the bodies of people lying on the ground, broken into pieces.

Christian looked at the broken bodies and asked.

"What does this mean?"

"Haven't you heard of those who fell into error because they listened to Hymenaeus and Philetus (2 Timothy 2:17-18), who said that the resurrection of the body had already passed away?"

"Yes, I have heard of them."

"These are the ones who fell to pieces at the bottom of this mountain, and as you can see, they have been left unburied to this day, so that others may be warned if they want to come near or climb the mountain.

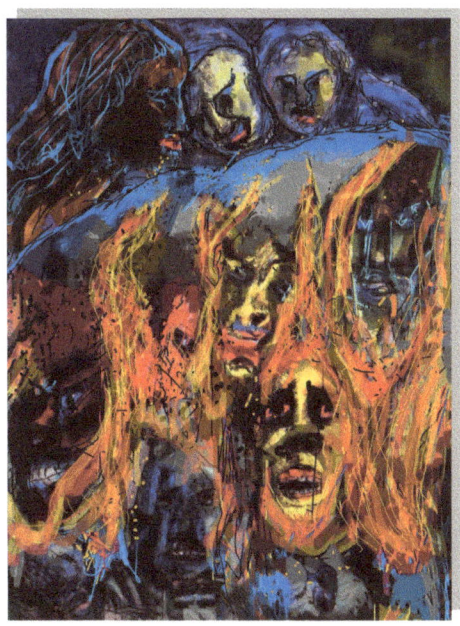

Top of the Error (2022)

The two pilgrims were led by shepherds on the road to Hell. In the distance they could hear the sound of burning fires, hear the cries of the tormented, and smell the sulfur. The shepherds' description of the place was wrong.

"This is the way to hell, the way of hypocrites: those who sell their birthright, like Esau; those who sell their teacher, like Judas; those who blaspheme the gospel, like Alexander; those who lie and cheat, like Ananias and his wife Sapphira."

Christian and Hopeful then said goodbye to the shepherds and entered the "province of pride. On a dark road they saw a man tied to seven strong ropes and being dragged by seven demons. The demons led him to a gate on the side of a hill that the pilgrims had seen before (Matt. 12:24; Prov. 5:22).

When Christian and Hopeful saw this, they were so frightened that they began to tremble. Christian thought the man being dragged by the demons was someone he knew, so he approached

The Seven Demons (2022)

him. Christian thought he looked like an "apostate" living in an "apostate village. But he turned his head the other way, like a thief caught in the act, so they couldn't get a good look at his face. Hopeful looked behind him after he had passed, and on his back was written, "Obscene Professor of Faith and Accursed Apostate.

We have seen many people who once believed in Jesus but were deceived by Satan and fell into the ways of the world.

What would be their end?

John Bunyan shows them being dragged away by seven demons and their end being in a pile of dead bodies at the pinnacle of error, with the sound of howling in agony and the smell of sulfur.

At times, our awareness and fear of the tortures of hell cause us to desire heaven fervently, but when our awareness of hell and fear of damnation diminishes, so does our zeal for heaven. In other words, we have a habit of going back to our comfortable ways when our consciousness and fear of sin diminishes, and so does our desire for heaven and happiness. This is why John Bunyan showed us the peak of error and the seven deadly sins. It's a sign for us not to stop our pilgrimage to heaven.

I climbed the Delectable Mountain of Joy and tried to talk to the animals I'd been putting off.

"Horrrr~, horrr~"

As I sang the song of the bush warbler, a male bush warbler came right up to me. From a naturalist's perspective, this is proof that he hears only sound and sees humans as competition. But from the creature's point of view, I've just revealed one of the secrets of its usual private conversations. So here's what I found on Delectable Mountain, a place where all kinds of mountain birds have conversations with secrets of their own.

Conversations with animals

"Do animals love like humans?

As an animal behaviorist, I ask myself this question. Do mother birds have motherly love for their young?

It's not an easy question to answer because, as a zoologist, I don't study the question in terms of human love. For example, a pair of swallows built a nest under the eaves and laid five eggs. Sometimes the mother doesn't lay them all at once, but one a day, or sometimes she lays them one day at a time. The young that hatches from the first egg is the largest, and the youngest is the smallest.

How can you tell?

You can tell by the size of their gaping yellow mouths. Here's a fun experiment to try. A mother bird will come in with a beak full of food, shovel it all into her largest open mouth, and then go on her next foraging trip. The next time she comes in with food, she'll shovel it into the second, the third, and so on. It's very regular. She doesn't duplicate the food she just ate, which raises a question.

Can the mother really tell them apart?

To find out, I made open-mouthed cubs out of cardboard and painted them bright yellow. They are all different sizes. We made one bigger than the oldest, one smaller than the youngest, and then when the mother swallow came in with food and all five of them opened their mouths at the same time, we put these fake beaks next to their snouts and a funny thing happened. The mother swallow would put food in the fake beak, which was bigger than her babies, but never in the tiny real swallow's mouth.

In nature, the mother swallow begins carrying food about two days after all five of her babies have hatched. During the first few days, the mother will feed about 80 times a day. She feeds the youngest with the widest open mouth, and after three to five minutes, she feeds the second. At this point, the first one is still in the feeding pouch, so it's not as hungry and doesn't open its mouth as wide. However, if the mother is late in bringing the food, a problem arises. Let's say there is a 20 minute delay. At the third turn, the first baby's mouth will be the widest again, and the third, fourth, and fifth babies will never get a chance to eat. That's pretty cruel.

If only the mother knew this, but God didn't give this swallow mother the wisdom to know this. To have that wisdom, the swallow's brain would have to be at least five or six times larger than it is now, just like a human's. That little brain just doesn't have the ability to discriminate. So in today's world, where the swallow's food source has been contaminated with pesticides and insecticides, and there's an absolute shortage of bugs, it's a struggle to raise two babies instead of five.

We see this as confirmation. God entrusted the care of creation to humans, not animals. The Bible attests to this fact.

> "Be fruitful and multiply, and replenish the earth and subdue it. And have dominion over the fish of the sea and over the birds of the air and over every living thing that moves on the earth (Genesis 1:28).

In this way, God gave man wisdom and empowered him to rule over living creatures, but man still doesn't understand all of God's words.

Baby Swallows (2018)

As a scientist, I often sense what God wants us to do. Of course, nature is often mysterious beyond its beauty, and the more we study it, the more unknown mysteries exist, so many scientists are still challenging the mysteries of nature. Trying to solve these mysteries brings a different kind of joy and pleasure.

Konrad Lorenz, who is called the father of animal behavior, won the Nobel Prize for studying the sounds and behavior of animals, so his book "Solomon's Ring" was introduced in Korea.

In the Old Testament, King Solomon is said to have talked to animals while wearing a ring. Of course, this story is only recorded in the Apocrypha. King Solomon is known as the king who asked God for wisdom, not wealth or power. We all know the story of the trial to determine the true mo Today I received a 10-week fetal ultrasound video from my daughter and she was excited to see the fetus moving inside her. I was excited too. I could see the head, the torso, the moving arms and hands, and I could hear the heart beating. I sent her a message of congratulations.

"God's handiwork at work!"

Whose handiwork is it to create a fetus?

Obviously, that fetus started as a single cell that fused together, and inside that cell are 46 chromosomes, all of which are present in every human being. Within those chromosomes, of course, is the genetic information that makes up the fetus. Biologically speaking, they're a double helix of sequences. They're like beads on a string.

A single cell divides over and over again to create a head, a brain, arms, legs, and organs.

How does a single cell do that?

As the cells differentiate, each cell does what it's supposed to do: some cells make heads, some make arms, some make legs, and so on.

Isn't that fascinating?

Cells contain the same genetic information on 46 chromosomes, but the cells that make arms are told (programmed) to make only arms, and the cells that make hands are told (programmed) to make only the specific parts of the hand.

Who determines this?

Today's science explains that it makes itself, commanded by genetic information, so just as a computer works because there is someone who programmed the information, there must be someone who programmed the genetic information in the fetus.

What's even more mysterious is that these cells communicate with each other. For example, the cells that make up the heart and the cells that make up the small intestine communicate with each other. At some point, the cells that make the heart say to the cells that make the small intestine.

"I'm going to make a heart, you make a small intestine!"

And vice versa, the cells in the small intestine say

"I'm only going to make small intestine, you make heart!"

If this communication didn't work, you might have two hearts or two or three small intestines. Scientists have already discovered that material exchange occurs across the cell membrane, which in turn acts on

Message to my daughter (2024)

regulatory genes in the nucleus that tell operational genes to make hands, feet, and organs.

Inside the mother's womb, the fetus collaborates in trillions of cell divisions over the course of 10 months. It's as if the universe came into being from a single ice cube, creating countless stars in the galaxy.

In his book *The Language of God*, Francis Collins describes this mystery of infallibility this way.

"This universe was created as if the various constants, from the gravitational constant to the weak nuclear force, had been set with an error of a hundred billionth of a part, as if they had been waiting for us to show up.

Yes, just as this universe was created without a single error, God is now creating a fetus in His daughter's body without a single error.

The good news is that God is already accomplishing far more than we could ever imagine, guess, or ask for in our wildest dreams, and that we are filled with His Spirit working deeply and gently within us, not forcing itself on us from the outside.

Talking to God

God wants to communicate directly with believers. The Bible is filled with examples of direct conversations with God. The Psalms are all records of conversations between the Psalmists, including David, and God. We've always thought of prayer as a one-way conversation with God, but if you look at Moses' interaction with God in the book of Exodus, it's a different story.

In a moment of desperation, with the Egyptian army closing in behind him and the Red Sea in front of him, Moses cries out to God.

"Lord, what shall I do? I am trying to lead the people according to your will, and the Red Sea is in my way. Please open a way for me.

God answered immediately.

The Lord said to Moses, "Why do you cry out to me, command the children of Israel to go forward, and take your staff and stretch out your hand over the sea and part it, and the children of Israel will walk on land in the middle of the sea..." (Exodus 14:15-18).

As I walked up the mountain today, I discovered a secret that makes this kind of communication possible, and that secret is Jesus. We can have a conversation with God through Jesus Christ.

We've been separated from God because of the sin of one man, Adam, and Jesus is the one who bridged that gap. The apostle Paul tells us this in the following words.

When Jesus died," he writes, "he brought sin down with him, and when he rose again, he brought God down to us. Paul again speaks to us: "God speaks to us Christians in our own language, and we do not miss a word" (Romans 6:11, The Massage).

The apostle Paul tells us that "this resurrection life that God has given us is not a timid or heavy life, but a life of adventure, full of anticipation," and that we should always ask God like a child.

"What's next, Dad?"

Once, while climbing a mountain, I was in a constant dialogue with God-not a one-way prayer, but a time of listening to His voice and asking questions. After such a time, I wondered.

"Oh, how come I didn't know God like this before?"

I realized that it was my sin that caused my separation from God, and that He took it all away so that I could have a conversation with Him again.

God speaks in spirit to the smallest movement of life. From this delicious mountain it is transmitted to my soul. Just as a bat emits ultrasonic waves inaudible to the human ear and lives to hear its echoes, so I tune into the voice of God, hear it, and run again toward the city of Zion.

CHAPTER 14

A LITTLE FAITH

Faith is invisible to us, and it doesn't happen just because we are ready to believe. I remember a chemistry experiment from my school days. There was a yellow liquid in a thin test tube. I used an eyedropper to put drops of yellow into the test tube. One drop, two drops... After five drops, nothing happened, but after the sixth drop, it turned red. The value at which the color changes is called the threshold. It's the same with grace. I've seen many people whose little faith didn't change color, but eventually, as they kept dropping drops of grace into the test tube, it turned into real faith. In The Threshold of Faith, John Bunyan portrays a man of little faith.

Christian and Hopeful were walking again. Suddenly a person came into Christian's mind.

"Mr. Hopeful, I suddenly remembered a nice man who lives near here."

His name was Little Faith and his hometown was Sincerity. Little Faith, who was on a pilgrimage with us, happened to be sitting there and fell asleep. Just then, three fierce thugs appeared on the road coming down from the wide gate, and their names were Faintheartedness, Unbelief, and Crime. When the thugs saw Little Faith, they sped up and came running. At that moment, Little Faith had just woken up and was about to start his pilgrimage. The thieves chased him and threatened him. Little Faith got scared and lost all his strength to run away. In the end, Little Faith was robbed of his money, beaten by the thieves, and fell down".

"Didn't they take all of Little Faith's possessions?"

"No. They did not search the place where he had hidden his jewels, so they were safe; but from what I have heard, the good man suffered a great deal, for he lost most of his livelihood."

"That is very remarkable indeed; and though the robbers left it out, is it not a wonder that little Faith hid it so well; for he was so discouraged when he saw them coming that he could not have exerted the strength and skill to hide anything.

"This is true, but the reason Little Faith did not lose this good thing is due more to good providence than to his own efforts.

Hopeful summed up Little Faith this way.

"Little Faith was a man of sincere but unfortunately fragile faith; he could be the faith of our neighbors who are not always alert and watchful, who are swayed by the ways the world offers them, who are plagued by Satan's manipulations, and who are prone to falling into his snares.

John Bunyan tells the story of Little Faith in the third person. This Little Faith is a character in a dialogue between Hopeful and a Christian. In fact, I think this Little Faith could be a reflection of many Christians.

When we go on pilgrimage, our own faith is often shaken. Just as Little Faith was robbed of his money by a thief, believers can be robbed of their confidence, peace and joy. Our faith is shaken because we have lost everything, but Little Faith, like all Christians, is a character who has been miraculously saved by God's infinite grace.

Little Faith (2022)

People of little faith

I have to admit that I'm a bit like the little man of faith in the Chronicles of Narnia. The Bible is full of examples of the little faith of Jesus' disciples.

The most prominent is Thomas, who refused to acknowledge Jesus' resurrection; he believed in Jesus only after touching the nail marks. To him Jesus said.

> "Do you believe because you have seen me? Blessed is the one who believes without seeing me.

Doubting Thomas (2023)

Peter was a man of little faith when he followed Jesus. Three times he denied that he knew Jesus, and when he walked on the troubled Sea of Galilee, it was only because he believed the Lord's words calling him out of the boat and onto the water that Peter was able to walk on the water for a short time. But Peter was only able to walk on the water for a short time because he saw the wind blowing on the sea and was afraid. When he fell into the water, Peter cried out.

"Lord, save me (Matt. 14:30)

"Immediately Jesus stretched out His hand and caught him" (Matt. 14:31) and rebuked him, "Why do you doubt?"

"O you of little faith, why do you doubt?" (Matt. 14:31)

O you of little faith! (2022)

The Lord tells us not to live in fear as the world does.

> "Do not be afraid, come and follow me. See where I am. Go out and preach the good news. For the kingdom of God is at hand, and there are many mansions in my house. Come, inherit the kingdom prepared for you from the foundation of the world."

As Christians, hardly a day goes by in our lives that we don't have internal and external fears, anxieties, worries, and distractions. These dark forces have crept into every corner of our world to the point where it's impossible to completely escape them. To me, who lives in such a world, Jesus says.

> "O you of little faith, why did you doubt?"

I can hear those words ringing in my ears as he spoke them to Peter that day.

One day it was morning. I got out of bed and painted a watercolor of a little man of faith from the Bible. The reason I drew him is because I was once like Nicodemus. In the Bible, Nicodemus wasn't even a non-believer in Jesus. He was a man who didn't fully accept Jesus because of his social status and prestige. But he came to Jesus at night and confessed.

> "Rabbi, we know that you are a teacher sent by God. No one can do these signs that you do unless God is with him. (John 3:2)

These words of Nicodemus led to a discussion with Jesus.

Jesus answered and said to him, "Truly, truly, I say to you, unless a man is born again, he cannot see the kingdom of God. Nicodemus said to him, "How can a man fly when he is old and born of a second womb? Jesus answered and said unto him, Verily, verily, I say unto thee, Except a man be born of water and of the Spirit, he cannot enter into the kingdom of God. That which is born of the flesh is flesh, and that which is born of the Spirit is spirit: marvel not therefore that I say unto thee, Thou must be born again. (John 3:1-7)

Nicodemus Finds Jesus (2022)

Nicodemus was a wealthy and prominent man of his day, and quite well known in Jerusalem. A Pharisee, he was already aware of the rumors that many people were following Jesus, which is why he chose to seek Him out at night, away from the public eye. As an intellectual, he probably knew the meaning of what Jesus was saying, but in that moment he acted like a fool: he admired Jesus and wanted to follow his words, but he was afraid of being labeled a follower.

I see myself in this Nicodemus. He had no intention of giving up his zoological research, stork restoration, teaching, and speaking engagements, even though they were more for my glory than God's.

Jesus comes to the center of my life

I had a colleague in physics; he was a man of integrity and reputation. I asked him if he believed in the existence of God.

"Do you know the German physicist Karl von Weizsäcker?"

I mentioned him partly because he was a physicist, but also because the president of Germany during my time abroad was his brother, Richard von Weizsäcker. He answered me.

"Karl von Weizsäcker was a world-renowned physicist and philosopher who did research on nuclear fusion inside stars" and "He was also at the Max Planck Institute in Göttingen, Germany, and he was a Protestant physicist."

This was told to me by a fellow physics professor via the now artificially intelligent web search. I was even more intrigued by what he said next.

"Of all the physicists who have won Nobel Prizes or are world famous, about half are of the Christian faith."

I was mildly surprised to learn that so many physicists with some of the best minds on the planet believe in the existence of God, because to my knowledge, far fewer of my colleagues who are natural scientists but who major in biology believe in the existence of God.

An indication that there are a surprising number of believers among physics majors in the natural sciences can be found in Dr. Stephen Hawking's usual media interviews. He is the physicist best known for his Big Bang theory. Although Dr. Hawking is a self-described atheist, he has been quoted as acknowledging the existence of God.

In a 2018 media interview before his death, a reporter asked Dr. Hawking.

"Do you believe there is a God?"

He refused to answer, and when the reporter asked him why, Hawking replied.

"Because if I said I believed there was a God, everyone would claim I believed in the same God they believed in."

Instead, he said, "I believe that the universe is governed by the laws of science," adding, "These laws must have been set by God. But God does not intervene to break those laws," he said, avoiding a direct answer and adding.

"The chances that something like the universe we live in came from something like the big bang are really small, so in that sense it's got a religious significance."

In another interview he said, "It would be hard to explain why the universe had to start this way, except that it was the handiwork of God, who decided to create beings like us."

"I am Alpha and Omega"

The Bible doesn't say when creation took place. Scientists believe that the universe is 13.8 billion years old, starting with the Big Bang. There's a star that was created just nine years after the Big Bang, and we call it the

Morning Star (Earendel), and it's about 12.9 billion light years away from Earth. This concept of time and space doesn't really have a precise description yet, other than "vast," although the Buddhist term "Yonggup" might be a closer approximation.

If we translate the time of the Big Bang into calendar time, we can get a relative idea of how big it is. Most importantly, when I realize that time and space, which we humans find vast, are "a moment" for God, I trust that His hand is touching my soul.

Let's turn back the clock 13.8 billion years from midnight on January 1, when the Big Bang occurred, to the creation of this planet we live on, Earth. In that time, more than 100 billion galaxies were created. The Earth we live on now is just one planet - a tiny star - in a solar system in a fringe galaxy called Andromeda.

The planet was created about 4.6 billion years ago, or the beginning of September by our calendar. The Bible says that life was first created on the same day that God began to create the heavens and the earth, which, if we extrapolate scientifically, means that life was first created on Earth 4 billion years ago, which is the middle of September.

And then we're only 3.5 million years away from the first appearance of primitive man on this planet, which is December 31st at 8:52 p.m. on the calendar, which is when the Bible says that on the sixth day God created man in his image.

After that, the earth grows in population through the concept of reproduction, and the first agriculture and the beginning of civilized life as we know it today is less than 10,000 years old. So this time is 30 seconds to midnight on December 31.

The time when God sent Jesus to save mankind is 2000 years ago, only six seconds before the stroke of midnight. Too late in God's vast concept of time to come to this tiny, tiny, tiny planet in a human body.

The apostle John, a disciple of Jesus, also tells us

> Of the Word of life (the Holy Spirit), which was from the beginning, which we have heard, which we have seen with our eyes, which we have looked upon, which we have noted, which we have touched with our hands, and which was made manifest, we have seen and testified, and we tell you of this eternal life (the Holy Spirit), which was with the Father and was made manifest to us" (1 John 1:1-2).

In the book of 1 John, the apostle John writes that he spent years talking to, seeing with his eyes, and touching with his hands Jesus, the One who generates eternal life (energy). He writes, "Jesus is eternal life itself, and he presides over the universe from heaven with life (energy).

When I think and meditate on the fact that the creation of the universe was not long ago and the Lord's coming to earth was only a few seconds ago, I feel the Holy Spirit working in me now. The Holy Spirit that was present 13.8 billion years ago when the universe was created or the Lord was present 2000 years ago is the same Holy Spirit, and He has transcended time to come to me now and hold me in His strong arms.

The apostle John says, "The Lord God Almighty, who is and who was and who is to come, says, 'I am Alpha and Omega'" (Rev. 1:8). We know from his spiritual insights and the revelation of the Bible that this universe had a beginning and will have an end.

Some scientists claim that this planet has about 100 million years left to live. Even 100 million years is a short time on the calendar, only two or three days, but the end of the world could come much sooner than that. As John Bunyan says in The Heavenly Road.

> "The day of the Lord will come like a thief in the night, in which the heavens will pass away with a great noise, the elements will be dissolved with fervent heat, and the earth and the works that are in it will be revealed (2 Peter 3:10).

Christian, the protagonist of John Bunyan's "The Passion of the Christ," went on a pilgrimage after reading this scripture. And I walk this pilgrimage, trusting that the Lord is close by my side, working in me through His Holy Spirit.

CHAPTER 15

ATHEIST AND IGNORANCE

We are nearing the end of The People of Heaven. John Bunyan presents both an atheist, who believes there is no heaven and opposes all religions, and an ignorant, who acknowledges the existence of God but lives a self-centered life.

While Hopeful and Christian look ahead, there is one person who is going in the wrong direction: Atheist.

"We're going to Mount Zion, where are you going?" Christian spoke to Atheist first.

"I was once like you, seeking the kingdom of heaven. But there is no such thing!"

"You must look beyond this world. The kingdom of heaven is beyond this world."

"I met a man named 'Ignorance' on the street, and he had some very interesting things to say about your religion. He said it's funny to think that believing in Christ is the way to the kingdom of heaven, because we can just say we believe and our lives can still be evil and we still go to heaven!"

After hearing Atheist's words, Hopeful continued.

"Did you say that his name is Ignorance? Ah- that is what he may say, but if he is a true Christian, he will prove it by his life. Some people may live their lives by the rules and rituals of religion, but at the end of time, such people will be thrown out at the gates of the kingdom. God knows who His children are.

Again, Christian said.

"The Bible says, 'Faith without works is dead' (James 2:26), not because our actions save us, but because real faith is fruitful in sincere behavior, so real faith fixes our lousy lives."

Hopeful adds.

"Yes, God is a searcher of the heart. Is God deceived by man's hypocrisy?"

After listening to Christian and Hopeful, the atheist scoffs at them and continues on his way.

"I too have come this far in search of heaven, but now I realize it's all in vain. So I'm going back to the path I once enjoyed, and I'll leave you to find your own heaven!"

Ignorance

There are ninety-two characters in the book, apart from the main character, Christian, and Ignorance speaks to Christian the most. John Bunyan considered Ignorance to be a very important character, and one that is often found around Christian. While the Atheist, as the name suggests, is someone who lives without acknowledging Christ as Saviour, Ignorance is someone who believes in Christ.

He describes his faith this way.

I believe that Christ died for sinners, and I believe that if I obey His laws, He will graciously accept me and release me from the curse and recognise me as a righteous people before God. I believe that God is willing to accept my efforts to fulfil my religious duties and to justify me in the light of Christ's merits.

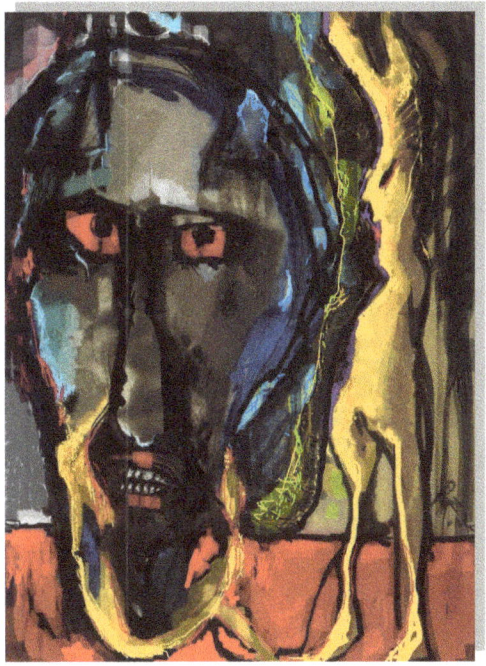

Atheist (2022)

This confession of Ignorance shows that he has a faith without substance. Not only that, but he has a false faith that seeks to be righteous apart from the personal righteousness of Christ. Ignorant faith makes Christ a works-justifier, not a person, and of course such a person will not escape the wrath of God on the Day of Judgment.

It is not uncommon to encounter such ignorant believers, even among those who hold very high positions in the Church. When someone demands an apology for humiliating them in front of others, they are reluctant to accept it because it is insincere.

'Elder, doesn't the Bible say to forgive seven times seven, even seventy times seven?'

The answer is quite surprising.

I cannot forgive you because your apology does not seem sincere to me, and the advice you have given me sounds like what Job's friend said to Job when he was suffering from bedsores.

I do not easily apologise to my brother either. And I often don't accept my brother's forgiveness, which is why I pray the Lord's Prayer every day: 'Forgive us our trespasses as we forgive those who trespass against us.

So I say to you. If you do not forgive your brother from the bottom of your heart, your heavenly Father will do the same to you" (Mt 18:35).

Ignorance finally reached the gates of heaven.

Instead of opening the gate, a man appeared on the threshold and asked.

Where do you come from and what do you want?

Ignorance replied.

I have eaten and drunk in the presence of my master, and he has taught us in the streets.

'And you have a certificate?

This question stunned Ignorance.

Then the devil picked him up, flew through the air to the door he had seen on the mountainside and threw him through it.

These words weigh more heavily on me today.

> It is not by saying 'Lord, Lord' that you will be able to come where I am. Only those who do the will of my Father will enter the kingdom of heaven (Matthew 7:21).

The devil sits Ignorance at the gates of heaven (2025)

Pilgrimage to St. Isidore 1

Whenever I visit Jeju Island, there is one place I always stop at. In my later years on Jeju Island, I walked the St. Isidore Pilgrim's Way for a while. When we think of pilgrimages, we think of the Camino de Santiago. I've visited Jeju Island many times like that, but I didn't know that Jeju Island had its own pilgrimage route.

It is said to be named after St. Isidore (Latin Isidorus), a farmer from Madrid, Spain, who is a Catholic saint (feast day, May 15).

There you'll find sculptures depicting the symbiotic love of Jesus from 2000 years ago.

The sculpture of Jesus on the eve of his crucifixion was so gruesome that you couldn't stand in front of it for long. It shows a living Jesus lying on a cross with a nail driven into the palm of his hand. On Jesus' face I could read the most excruciating pain a human being could ever suffer. There was also a scene where a soldier, in a fit of fever, prevented a woman from reaching Jesus.

What would you have done if you had been there 2000 years ago?

I probably would have fainted right there, because I don't usually watch gory scenes.

The Cross of Jesus and the Two Prisoners (2022)

As I walked the Isidore pilgrimage, my eyes were drawn to the scene of Jesus' crucifixion between two prisoners. More than 2,000 years ago, the Lord hung on a cross on Calvary with two other prisoners. The Bible records the scene as follows.

"Two other prisoners were also led away with Jesus to be killed. When they came to a place called Calvary, they crucified Him. They nailed one to His right side and the other to His left. Jesus prayed. "Father, forgive these men. They don't know what they are doing." (...)

Above Jesus' head was a sign that said, "This is the King of the Jews. One of the prisoners running with him also cursed him. "You are a great Messiah, aren't you? Save us! Save us!" But another prisoner interrupted him. "Are you not afraid of God? He suffers the same as you. We deserve to be punished, but he does not. He hasn't done anything to deserve this punishment." Then he said, "Jesus, enter your kingdom. "Jesus, remember me when you enter your kingdom," said Jesus. "Don't worry. I will do it. Today you will be with me in paradise." Now it was noon. The whole earth went dark, and it stayed dark for the next three hours. It was pitch black. The veil of the temple was torn in the middle. Jesus cried out in a loud voice. "Father, into your hands I commend my life!" And having said this, He breathed His last (Luke 23:32-46)."

Am I really giving myself to Jesus like a prisoner?

I think to myself. What matters to me now is that the moment I believe that Jesus died on the cross for my sins, I receive new life.

How is this possible?

In a way, it seems so unfair. I've been a prisoner all my life, and all it takes is one moment and one confession to go to heaven?

Secular religions believe that deep repentance, community service, or doing many good deeds will get you into paradise. But Christianity doesn't believe that - all you have to do is realize that, like the thief on the cross with Jesus, you can go to heaven with a single moment of confession.

John Bunyan's "Little Faith" in The Passion of the Christ lived a shaky life in the world, but he had faith in God, not in his own merits, so he confessed.

"Thank you, God, for giving me faith in your Son, who loved me and gave his life for me."

With this confession, I left the shrine of the crucifixion and went to the scene where the body of Jesus, who had just died on the cross, was being carried by a man named Joseph of Arimathea. As I stood in front of the scene, a number of thoughts came to my mind.

"Jesus is crucified and that's it," I thought, "He's just going to go down in history as a saint!"

The reason I thought this was because the image of Jesus as a dead man was so different from the image of Jesus as a king coming to save the world.

People Carrying the Body of Jesus (2022)

But then the story takes a turn. On the third day, Jesus rose from the dead. After three days, biologically speaking, a body begins to decompose, but Jesus appeared to his disciple Thomas in one piece, holding out his hand to show him the nail marks. He also visited Peter, the disciple who had followed him, and ate with him. He also appeared to the disciples on the road to Emmaus. The Bible records that Jesus spent 40 days with his disciples and then ascended into heaven before them.

But his ascension didn't end there. He challenged his disciples to live the same life he had lived, and he didn't just challenge them with words. He came upon them in the Holy Spirit as they gathered in the Upper Room at Pentecost. This is the work and grace of the Holy Spirit, sent by God, alive and well, beyond the understanding of a natural scientist's reason and knowledge. As each of these scenes is transferred to the page, I feel my soul being touched by the Holy Spirit and grace.

The Risen Jesus and Peter (2022)

Jesus ascends to heaven before His disciples (2022)

CHAPTER 16

THE LAND OF BEULAH

The great reality that looms like a mountain over the reality in which we live is the fact that "God is love"-that God loves this world. This love permeates every detail of the reality we encounter and deal with on a daily basis. His supreme love is found in the land of "Beulah" (Isaiah 62:4). A phrase from worldly life comes to mind for a moment.
"If I were to die tomorrow, I would have nothing left."
I honestly don't like this saying, but as long as I am walking in this "land of Beulah" right now, there is nothing like it, because I know that God loves me and all of us so much.

The two pilgrims entered a magical land, and strangely enough, drowsiness overcame them, for this was a land that the "shepherds" had warned them to be careful of, and so they held back their drowsiness and entered the land of Perla.

There the birds were singing all the time, the ground was covered with flowers, and the doves were cooing. In this land, the sun shone day and night. This was the borderland of heaven, and the pilgrims enjoyed sweet rest. And they heard a loud voice from heaven.

"Say to your daughter Zion. Behold, your salvation has come; behold, your reward is with him, and your reward is before him" (Isa. 62:11).

People of the Land of Beulah (2023)

At last the gates of heaven came before them, and before them was a river with rushing waters. Suddenly they heard the voice of an angel saying.

"We must cross the river of death to reach the gates of heaven. It's the last gate before we reach the gates of heaven?

Christian asked.

"I can't see anything, so how am I supposed to cross it? Shouldn't I choose a good place to cross and make some plans on how to do it...and is there a way back?"

Again the angel replied.

"You will not see the river until you set foot on it, and there is no way back; it is the way you must go".

Holy Ecstasy

I was entering the twilight of my life, a time when, as a Christian, I needed rest and spiritual replenishment in the land of Perla. As I slowly made my way along the pilgrimage path, I saw two pheasants in the leafy Zelkova trees competing for mates. It was an ecstatic moment in the life of a single creature.

Modern scientists, especially animal behaviorists, explain it as an interaction between external and internal stimuli: hormones. Even now, this planet called Earth spins around the sun at speeds of over 100,000 kilometers per hour, and it hasn't stopped since the heavens and the earth were created.

As they get closer to the sun, the amount of light gradually increases, and this light stimulates the pituitary gland through the gerbil's visual system (eyes). The pituitary gland releases gonadotropins through thin blood vessels. This hormone reaches the genitals and causes the release of sex hormones. Scientists call these hormones "gonadotropins. This vocalization hormone causes males to sing.

When females hear this song, they are ready to mate with the male and are also interested in building a nest. At this point, the female's body releases hormones that lead to ecstasy, a process that takes place as the male and female compete for supremacy. The female releases prolactin, a hormone that makes her want to build another nest, and her breast feathers are shed, revealing bare skin. At this point, the mother lays her eggs and places her bare, featherless skin against the warmth of her mother's body. All the while, we are unaware of the ecstasy that is taking place inside the bodies of these birds.

Flowers and Birds in the Land of Beulah (2016)

This has been happening since the beginning of time when God created these creatures. In the Bible's Song of Songs, we can read of the ecstasy of God's supreme love for the earth.

The winter is past, the rain has ceased, the ground is blossoming, the birds are singing, the voice of the dove is heard in our land; the fig tree is ripe with green fruit, the vine is in bloom and gives off its fragrance; arise, my beloved, my beautiful one, and let us go together" (Song 2:11-13).

God's love is like that, so extreme and delicate.

I saw a small bird slip through a crack in the stone of a retaining wall in the mountains. It's a tiny space, so tiny that no one would notice it, not even the nearby bobcats. The bird, barely the size of an adult thumb, held a piece of blue lichen in its beak. It soon disappeared through the crevice, leaving only its eyes, the size of a grain of rice, shining through the stone.

The piece of blue moss helps regulate humidity for the chicks that will soon emerge from the egg.

Scientists call it "naturally adaptive behavior," just as we keep a humidifier on in the room where a baby sleeps during the dry season. God loves these tiny creatures so much that He created them and gave them this wisdom.

In his book, Birds Our Teachers, John Stott, an English theologian and famous preacher, writes that we learn faith by watching God feed the crow, repentance by watching the stork migrate, freedom by watching the eagle soar, and joy by listening to the lark sing.

In the hermaphrodite of the grackle, I see Adam and Eve when sin had not yet entered the earth.

One day, sin entered this planet, and the Bible, through the Apostle Paul, tells us that it was Adam who brought sin to this planet.

He writes, "One man sinned, and so we all fell into the same predicament of sin and death" (Romans 5:18, The Message).

We were cut off from the heavenly kingdom that God created in the beginning, and it is Jesus Christ who will restore that connection. In this moment, as we walk the pilgrimage of life, we encounter the One who broke that separation and gave his love so generously for us.

Pilgrimage to St. Isidore 2

As I walked along the pilgrimage route to St. Isidore, my steps stopped in front of the scene of Jesus' symbiotic love that opened the eyes of a blind man. In front of the sculpture, I opened my sketchbook and captured an event from 2,000 years ago when the Lord healed the sick (John 9:1-7).

When Jesus saw the blind man, he spat on the dirt, kneaded clay, put it on the man's eyes and said.

"Go to the pool of Siloam and wash."

He did as he was told, and the man received his sight. This is a sign that Jesus is the Son of God.

Jesus could not have done this.

According to the Bible, this blind man was born blind. He didn't have glaucoma or cataracts like we see today. He was born with a congenital defect somewhere in the nerve cells of his retina, so he was beyond the reach of modern medicine, and Jesus told him to put spit on his eyes and then go to a pool to wash.

Jesus Heals the Blind Man (2023)

When the disciples saw this man who had been blind from birth, they came to Jesus and asked him a question.

> "Teacher, whose sin was it that made this man blind, his own or his parents'?" (John 9:2)

Jesus gave an unexpected answer to the question of why he was blind.

> "This man did not sin, nor did his parents. It's just that God is revealing the things He is doing in him" (John 9:3-5).

In this way, Jesus explained that the man's blindness was not a punishment for a specific sin, but rather to introduce people to Jesus, who is the glory and light of God.

The Bible (Mark 5:25-34) tells of a woman who had been bleeding for 12 years. She believed that if she touched the hem of Jesus' garment, she would be healed.

Today, as I painted 'The Woman with the Hemorrhage' (2022) in watercolour on Korean paper, I prayed.

"Lord, right now I am struggling with a serious illness.

"Please don't turn away from me!"

As I looked at Jesus' healing work in the Bible, I had a question I wanted to ask the Lord.

The Woman with the Hemorrhage (2022)

"Lord, can you give me this kind of healing power?

The answer to this question was found in the Bible, because on the day of Pentecost, after Jesus ascended to heaven, when the disciples gathered in the upper room and prayed fervently, this power was given. We believe that we can receive healing power just like the disciples did by praying and asking. But when we look at the purpose of Jesus' miracles, He didn't just heal the sick.

We see this in Jesus' answer to his disciples' question about why a man was blind. Jesus healed to reveal the existence of God and His glory.

Washing the Disciples' Feet (2024)

"I have washed your feet and now you must wash your neighbor's feet. I have set an example for you, so you must do exactly as I have done. If you know what I mean, you should do the same. Have a blessed life" (John 13:13-17).

Jesus himself modeled this humble Christian life.

As I was painting and writing Washing the Disciples' Feet, I learned that I had prostate cancer growing in my body. I was diagnosed with terminal cancer and suddenly I thought to myself.

"Now my body is one step closer to the river of death!

The fact is that if you develop prostate cancer in old age, you have a 25% chance of dying from it. That means the other 75% will die of something else. It was somewhat expected, so I couldn't just wallow in sadness.

> "I am dying daily" (1 Corinthians 15:31)"

> "Present your bodies a living sacrifice, holy and pleasing to God, which is your reasonable service. This is your spiritual worship, your spiritual service (Romans 12:1)."

The Apostle Paul tells us in 2 Corinthians (5:9-10)

> "Our hope is to be people who are pleasing to the Lord, for we must all appear before the judgment seat of Christ, so that each one may receive what is due to him, according to what he has done in the body, whether good or bad."

Henri J.M. Nouwen, seeing the Lord kneeling before us, wrote

> "Only through union with the body of Christ do I know the full meaning of my body. My body is much more than a fleeting instrument of pleasure and pain. My body is the house in which God intends to reveal the full glory of his divinity. Therefore, caring for our bodies and the bodies of others is a truly spiritual act. For it brings our bodies closer to the glorious experience.

Christian Love

The Lord has a special love for me as I live my limited life on this final pilgrimage. He tells us to "love your neighbor more than yourself," which is why we Christians rank love above faith, hope, and charity among the Christian virtues of faith, hope, and charity.

People mistakenly think that being compassionate is all there is to love. Of course, a compassionate heart is important, but it can be overemphasized, which is controversial. In Mere Christianity, C.S. Lewis, the greatest Christian apologist of our time, defines Christian love as follows.

> "Love for ourselves is a state of the will, not a state of emotion; we have it instinctively, but love for others must be learned and cultivated.
>
> If you're a Christian, you need to pause here and heed his words.
>
> For Christians, love is a matter of the will. As we strive to do God's will, we are obeying the command to "love the Lord your God" (Matt. 22:37-38). God will give us the emotion of love if He chooses, but we cannot create this emotion on our own, nor do we have the right to demand it. But the important thing to remember is that our emotions come and go, but God's love for us never does.
>
> -C.S. Lewis, Mere Christianity-

So what does God's love look like? The Bible tells us to love our enemies. Loving our enemies is a difficult thing to put into practice.

What reward have you if you love those who love you; and if you do it to your brother, what reward have you above all men; and if you do it to the Gentiles, what reward have you above all men (Matthew 5:46-47)?

But if you think the river of death is right in front of you, it's different.

Why, why not?

Because God is love, even in death.

For we live in this tabernacle, and we groan, because we are weighed down with a heavy burden; and we do not want to be undressed, but to be strapped. So that death may be swallowed up by life (2 Corinthians 5:4-5).

I am reminded of a line from a poem by Yoon Dong-joo, a Christian poet.

'I must love what is dying.'

He was born during the Japanese occupation of Korea, and although he was tortured to death in prison, he left us a beautiful poem about God's love, or eternal life, while facing the river of death.

We say that we are blessed if we can live a long time without dying, but in fact God is not so much interested in how long we live as in how long we die.

Genesis 4 tells the story of Cain and his brother Abel.

Abel was a shepherd who tended sheep, and Cain was a farmer who ploughed fields. After many years, Cain offered to the Lord the grain of the earth, and Abel offered the fat of the firstborn of the flock (Gen 4:2-4).

But the Lord was pleased with Abel and his offering, but not with Cain and his offering.

Finally, Cain became very angry and struck down his brother Abel.

When I read the book of Genesis, I couldn't understand this story.

Why would God send Abel, whom he had honoured with a sacrifice, to an early death?

In the New Testament, John the Baptist was praised by Jesus as the greatest a woman had ever given birth to (Matthew 11:11), but he was killed by Herod before Jesus (Mark 6:17-28).

The God who loves us does not care how long we live on this earth.

For we know that if our earthly house of tabernacles is destroyed, we have a building from God, a house not made with hands, eternal in the heavens, not made with human hands," wrote Paul (2 Corinthians 5:1).

In the face of the river of death, God is still giving grace and creating new life in me. This life is but a small thing compared to the great feast that God has prepared for us. For what we see is here today and will be gone tomorrow, but what we do not see will last forever.

CHAPTER 17

THE RIVER OF DEATH

Is there a line between life and death? If so, what is the distance between life and death? John Bunyan, author of Pilgrim's Progress, identified the river of death as the boundary. In reality, there is no boundary, only a biological one. When we humans deal with someone on their deathbed, we think of the moment when the breath stops and the head drops as the boundary between life and death. For God, there is no boundary, and He didn't create it. He made it so that the new life in my body can continue by living and believing. Jesus confirmed this with His resurrection on the cross and His promise to come again.

Finally, Christian and Hopeful have reached the river of death. Christian speaks first.

"But I can't see, I can't see an inch."

"Brother Christian, let the faith of Christ bring peace to your heart, He will get you across, you can't try to do it yourself."

The river was churning again with strong winds and violent waves. Their conversation became urgent.

"Christian! Christian, this is the river of death, we have to cross it, there is no other way."

"Hopeful~! Hopeful~! I'm sinking! I can't cross!"

"No, Brother Christian, I can feel the ground under me, we can cross!"

"I see the door there. I feel the weight of my sins! My sins are sinking me, I can't do it!"

"No, Christian, the burden of your sins is already gone, open your eyes and look, you can cross!"

"No, it's too deep, I'm abandoned, my sins must be too great!"

"You are a new creature, look, God is waiting for you, He promised you."

"That... yes, I see it again. I see the other side, there! There!"

And so the two pilgrims crossed the river of death and arrived safely at the gates of heaven.

Two angels greeted them.

"Welcome, welcome, we will now escort you to heaven."

"But how do we get to this high heaven?"

"It does not matter to you now how high or low the hill to heaven is, for you have already left your bodies in the river."

When Christian and Hopeful heard this, their hearts leapt. They really didn't feel the weight of their flesh.

Two Pilgrims Cross the River of Death (2022)

The Death of the Stork Furmi

I think of Furmi, the stork who died next to me at the River of Death. As a zoologist, it's not easy to see animals die in the wild, which means we find their bodies, but rarely see them on their deathbed.

When Furmi was donated to us by the World Bird Park in Walsrode, Germany, it was around the time I started working with storks. They gave us four breeding birds and sent us the oldest male, Furmi, who was well over 25 years old at the time. With an average lifespan of 30 years, he was an old stork.

He was brought to Germany as a chick from the Amur nature reserve in Russia. At that time, the Walssrode Bird Park in Germany had imported the globally endangered Class 1 protected Korean Stork from Russia and had already achieved success in captive breeding before us. It was used as a breeding bird, so it came to Germany as an old bird.

When she was 28 years old, her food intake decreased in the winter and she was unable to climb up to a one-meter torch pole. Especially in cold weather, when the temperature dropped below minus 10 degrees Celsius, she often sat on the floor because she was weak from lack of food. So she had to live with a heater in the winter. Even so, she no longer had the strength to survive, and we realized she was dying 20 days before her death when her food intake was noticeably lower than normal.

She was missing a lot of feathers, and the muscle mass hidden by the feathers had shrunk to the point where you could feel nothing but bone when you touched her. The week before it died, it had barely eaten - or perhaps it's more accurate to say it had stopped eating altogether - and slumped to one side of the aviary with its long legs crossed, waiting to die.

A day before he died, his head began to hang down. He showed no resistance when I entered his cage and touched his body. Six hours before he died, I saw his eyes close repeatedly as he breathed heavily. In the end, Fumi died at the age of 32. In human years, she would have been about 80.

Farewell to Furmi the Stork (2016)

"Will I die like Furmi?

This is a question I've been asking myself more and more as I stare down the river of death. It's probably a sign of my age, but it's also because more and more people around me are living with dementia and being cared for by nurses.

Regardless, it seems clear that these days, how we die is more important than how we are born.

As I live with these thoughts, a verse from the Bible becomes a fervent prayer.

> "They have no pain in death, and their strength is strong; they have no sorrow like others, and no calamity like others" (Psalm 73:4-5).

Perhaps John Bunyan included hope in River of Death because he wanted Christians to live with hope.

The apostle Paul, who wrote that sin had made death a fearful thing, was surely right when he said that through the one victory of the One who is life, both sin and death have been abolished.

> "We give thanks to God who gives us the victory through our Lord Jesus Christ" (1 Corinthians 15:57).

It was time to take His life into my body, so I made the pilgrimage to Isidore, the last castle, facing the river of death, with only my eyes on the One who redeemed me.

Jesus on a donkey

On the pilgrimage to Ishdol, the last city, we come across a sculpture of Jesus entering Jerusalem on a donkey before his crucifixion.

When Jesus rode into Jerusalem on a donkey with a large crowd, it was Passover. Passover was a celebration of God's deliverance of Israel from slavery in Egypt, so the Jewish hope for future deliverance from their current troubles was very strong at that time of year, and Rome had troops stationed in Jerusalem in case there was a need to quell unrest. By treating Jesus as the object of this hope, the crowds began to realize that this teacher was the Messiah who could lead them against Rome.

Jesus on the Donkey (2022)

Surrounded by a crowd shouting "Hosanna!" Jesus seemed to be focused on something else entirely. He didn't look at the excited crowd; he didn't wave; he looked beyond the noise and excitement and saw what lay ahead: an agonizing journey that would lead to betrayal, torture, crucifixion, and death.

For Jesus, there was also a calm acceptance. There was insight into the fickleness of the human heart, but there was also an overflowing compassion. Above all, there was the presence of love. He had a boundless love born of unbreakable intimacy with God.

It was a love that was infinitely deep and infinitely wide, reaching out to everyone in the whole world. There was nothing He did not fully know, and there was no one He did not fully love.

Every time I see Christ on the donkey, I feel that He sees all my sins, guilt, and shame, and I am reminded that He loves me with all His forgiveness, mercy, and compassion.

As I walk my pilgrimage, I intend to live a life of complete obedience to His Word.

You see a colt tied up and no one has ridden him; untie him and bring him to me. And if anyone asks you how to untie it, say to him, 'The Lord will use it'" (Luke 19:30-31);

With these words, I decided to give to the Lord what I still held in my hands, and I went over to where the statue of the risen Jesus stood.

His crucifixion was carried out in three days, as prophesied in the Bible. For forty days after his resurrection, Jesus did not appear to Annas, Caiaphas, Herod, or Pilate, who had condemned him to death, nor to Nicodemus, his rebellious disciple, nor to Joseph of Arimathea, who buried him.

"I was right, wasn't I?"

"Didn't I always say that?"

He didn't say those things. Nowhere in the Bible do we find him saying these things. His interactions with them were simply events hidden deep in time.

Mary Magdalene saw a stranger in the garden. Globus and his friend walked with a stranger on the road to Emmaus. The disciples saw a stranger and thought it was a ghost. Peter, Thomas, Nathanael, John, James, and two other disciples heard the voice of a stranger calling to them at the lake. Jesus was that stranger.

The Risen Jesus (20-22)

The people of Emmaus

They returned to their hometown dejected and disillusioned. They had been oppressed for so long under Roman rule. They had never known true freedom, only a vague longing for it. So when they met Jesus, they were full of hope.

They hoped that this man from Nazareth would bring them the freedom for which they had longed for so many years. But it was all in vain, for the man they had hoped for was arrested by the Romans, condemned to death, and crucified. Fearing that his body would be lost, they took a large stone and sealed the tomb.

The three days that Jesus was in the tomb represented the decay of the body. Therefore, Globa and her friend on the road to Emmaus believed that there was nothing they could do to prevent Jesus' death, and they were deeply desperate. In this despair, they set out on the road to Emmaus. When they came upon Jesus, he became like a wild animal, but they did not recognize him.

Jesus Talking to Two People on the Road to Emmaus (2022)

Jesus saw through the desperation of these two men. Jesus knew from experience what human despair is. He knew death and the grave, and he knew our finiteness. Globa and her friend must have sensed that this stranger was not a stranger; he knew them too well to remain a stranger for long. They knew that he was not trying to offer them the false comfort of a "worldly wise man.

Jesus shows us from His experience that life is stronger and greater than death and decay. This is something that only the heart can understand. Luke, the author of the Gospel of Luke, doesn't write "they understood" or "saw the light". He puts it more emphatically.

"Their hearts were burning within them (Luke 24:32).

This burning in their hearts showed Globa and her friend something completely new. Something at the very heart of existence, at the very center of human existence, had disarmed death and neutralized despair. It was not simply a new perspective, a new joy of life, a new confidence; it was what can only be described as a new life, a new soul.

A modern way of describing what happened to the two men on the road to Emmaus would be this.

Spiritual life, or spirituality, began in their hearts.

Globa and her friend asked this stranger to come into their home and eat with them. As they sat down to eat, he took bread, blessed it, and broke it for them. Then they suddenly realized with unshakable conviction that this was Jesus, the one who had died and been buried in the tomb. But just as this conviction had set in, he disappeared from their sight.

Globa and His Friend (2023)

Something so profound had happened. The moment Globa and her friend recognized Jesus in the breaking of the bread, they no longer needed His physical presence as a condition for their new hope. Their relationship with Jesus had become so intimate that His strangeness had been wiped away. They no longer needed His physical manifestation as a basis for hope because He was so close. As they talked with Him on the road, they realized two things.

The first was that the new life that had been born would never leave them, and the second was that He would give them the strength to return to Jerusalem and tell others why all was "not finished. So Luke records that they immediately returned to Jerusalem and told their experience to the eleven disciples and those who were with them.

I am in the middle of my own journey and I am facing the river of death. I am facing death, but through faith in the resurrection of Jesus, I am living a life of wholeness, a life of healing, a life of inclusion.

What God did for His Son Jesus, He does for us. Through the indwelling Holy Spirit, He brings us back to life, just like the body of Christ (Romans 8:11).

When He died, just as sin died, He rose again, promising us eternal life. So Jesus Christ lives with us today in this body, but the "river of death" that lies before us is just the process of washing away the body.

Now it is clearer to me that the resurrection of our bodies and eternal life await us Christians through Jesus Christ. Therefore, today I walk silently but boldly on the journey of the heavenly way.

BIBLIOGRAPHY

The Complete Bible (2003). Standard New Translation Revised Edition. Korean Bible Society
The NIV Korean-English Study Bible (2004). Word of Life Press, Seoul.
The Message New Testament (2014). The Message: the New Testament (E.H. Peterson). Translated by Soohyun Kim, Jongseok Yoon, and Jongtae Lee. The Blessed
The Message: the Old Testament (2013). The Message: the Old Testament (E. H. Peterson). Translated by Jongtae Lee. Blessed Man
Pilgrim's Progress (2022) (J. Bunyan). Translated by Hoon Choi. Poem
Pilgrim's Progress (2018) (J. Bunyan). Translated by Yoo Seong-Deok. CH Book
Pilgrim's Progress (2020)(J. Bunyan). Translated by Youngho Park. CLC
Pilgrim's Progress Walking with Dongwon Lee (2016). Lee, Dongwon. Duranno
The Bible Background Commentary (2010). (J.H. Walton, V.H. Matthews, M.W. Chavalas & C.S. Keener). IVP
Visionary Bible Dictionary (2001). Yongjo Ha. Duranno.
Beginning Christian (2016). Sanghak Lee. Duranno.
Jesus, Our Gospel (2006). (H.J.M. Nouwen). Translated by Jongseok Yoon. The Blessed

Mere Christianity (2014). (C.S. Lewis). Translated by Jang Kyung-Cheol Jong-Tae. Hongsungsa

Paul the Apostle (2009). Paul the Apostle (J. Pollock). Translated by Jongrak Hong. Hongsungsa

Jesus the Apostle (2019). Lee Chul-hwan. Lifebook

Tim Keller, The Reason for God (2023). The Reason for God (T.Keller). Translated by Cho,Jong-Hoon. Duranno

Ants (2001). Les Fourmis (B. Werer) translated by Sewook Lee. Open books

The Language of God (2007). The Language of God: A Scientist Presents Evidence for Belief (Frencis S. Colin) translated by Changshin Lee.

The Birds Our Teachers (2001). The Birds Our Teachers (J. Stott). Translated by Lee Gibbon, IVP

Solomon's Ring (2000): He Talked with Cattle, Birds, and Fish (K. Lorenz). Translated by Gimchee Kim. Science Books

Sociobiology (1992). Sociobiogoy (E.O. Wilson) translated by Byung-Hoon Lee, Si-Ryong Park. Minumsa

After the Widow Stork (2004). Korea Stork Restoration Research

ILLUSTRATIONS

Chapter 1.

1. What the heck am I supposed to do?(2023): A wanderer was wandering through the wilderness of the world and came to a cave with a book in his hand and a heavy burden on his back. He opened the book and began to read. When he finished, he was shaking with tears. Later, as if he couldn't stand it anymore, he said out loud, "What the hell am I going to do?
2. The Neighborhood Brother (2016): Where we lived was a steep cul-de-sac with a broken cement staircase, and the houses were tightly packed on either side of the staircase. One day I caught my sister pulling out some of my mom's saved clothes and meeting her older brother upstairs.
3. The Child Jesus (2021): For me, Jesus' childhood was also a time of great curiosity, but there is only one appearance of his childhood in the Bible. He's in a heated discussion with the rabbis in the temple (Luke 2:41-52). It's clear from this picture of Jesus as a child that he was just an extraordinary man, not the Son of God.
4. Jesus overcomes the temptations of the devil (20-23): The Bible does not tell the story of Jesus' upbringing; all we know is that he

grew into a young man of about 30 years of age, was baptized by John the Baptist, fasted for 40 days in the wilderness, and overcame the temptations of the devil. He lived a short symbiotic existence on this earth of three years.

5. The Family of the Madman (2005): My father used to come home drunk, and on those days he became a madman; once he started drinking to excess, he was not a normal person. On days when he came home late drunk, he would wake up the rest of the family. I was so afraid of my father who had become a madman.

Chapter 2

1. Stubbornness (center) and Fickleness (right) (2022): When Christian left the city of destruction, there were two people who followed him: Stubbornness and Fickleness. Stubbornness stopped Christian and asked him why he was leaving his hometown.
2. The Swamp of Discouragement (2022): Fickleness stomped out of the swamp, shouted, "No, is this the happy life you promised me for this pilgrimage?" and turned back the way he came, never looking back. Christian barely escaped the swamp, thanks to the help of an evangelist who happened to be passing by.
3. Christian at the entrance to Moral Village (2022): Suddenly, Christian sees a fire roaring up the hill, and he fears that if he climbs up, he will be caught in the flames and burned to death. He begins to sweat and tremble with fear. Finally, Christian begins to regret having accepted the wrong advice from the worldly wise man.
4. Secular Wise Men (2022): While attending church, I met secular wise men in my academic world, first Charles Darwin of the theory

of evolution, and then Richard Dawkinson, author of The Selfish Gene.

5. The Miracle of the Five-Footer (2020): Jesus said (John 6:10-13). "Let the people be seated." And they sat down, and there were about five thousand people. Jesus took the loaves, gave thanks, and distributed them to those who were seated; and he did the same with the fish; and the people were filled, and there were twelve small loaves left over.

Chapter 3

1. The Narrow Gate (2022): Christian knocked at the narrow gate without hesitation, and "Goodwill" opened the door and asked, "Whom do you seek?" "Yes, I am leaving the city of destruction and making my way to Mount Zion. Will you take in sinners like me?" The Christian said, and with all his heart, Goodwill shared the Bible (John 6:37), "All that the Father gives me will come to me, and the one who comes to me I will never cast out.

2. Goodwill and Christianity (2022): Do you see the narrow way that stretches out in the distance? This is the way you should go from now on; the way your fathers and many prophets, Christ and his disciples, made straight as a ruler, and this is the way you should go from now on.

3. The Korean Stork's Nest (2019): Long before the Korean people lived in the land of the Korean peninsula, they bred in the marshes along the Amur River in Russia. When they found a beautiful marsh in the land of the east, one or two birds began to descend and built a nest near a private house.

4. Silence in the Dark (2015): "Ah, God made that sound in the beginning," long before man walked the earth. The Bible says, "Eye

hath not seen, nor ear heard, neither have entered into the heart of man, the things which God hath prepared for them that love him" (1 Corinthians 2:9).
5. Earth Spacecraft (2022): In the beginning, God created everything in the universe, and inside the spaceship called Earth, He created the plants and animals and the first passenger, Adam.

Chapter 4

1. The Interpreter and the Christian (2022): A well-meaning man came to the interpreter's house with a scroll in his hand and said, "I am a stranger from the city of destruction, and I am here because a man who is well acquainted with the master of this house told me to come to him and that he would show me something profitable.
2. The Waterer and the Broom (2022): This room represents the human heart that has never been sanctified by the sweet grace of the gospel. The dust represents man's original sin and the corruption that makes every man that way. The man who first began to sweep this room is the law, and the woman who next sprinkled water on it is the gospel.
3. Desire and Patience (2022): Desire symbolizes man in this world, and patience symbolizes man in the hereafter. As we have just seen here, desire wants to have everything in this world right now, and similarly, the people of this world want to have everything they can get their hands on right now, and they cannot wait until the world to come.
4. Anointing and watering (2022): This fire represents grace working in the heart of man. It is the devil who tries to extinguish the fire by throwing water on it, but the fire still burns more and more intensely.

5. Paul of Damascus (2022): "Saul, Saul, why do you seek to harm me?" "Lord, who are you?" "I am Jesus, whom you persecute."(Acts 9:1-5)

Chapter 5

1. Simple (right) Lazy (middle) Arrogant (left) (2022): Christian sees the three pilgrims and tries to help them out of their stuck state, but their responses are all apathetic: "I don't feel any danger or anything, it's just a nice life the way it is" (Simplicity), "I think I'll just rest here for a bit and chat" (Sloth), "People are all going about their business. Mind your own business" (Arrogance)
2. Courtesy and Hypocrisy (2022): From the other side of a narrow street, you see two people jumping over a wall on your left. One was Courtesy and the other was Hypocrisy.
3. Ants (2019): Professor Wilson, author of Sociobiology, was a world-renowned scholar who did his Ph.D. on ants. He was generally irreligious, and his influence, the ant novelist Berber, wrote a seemingly cynical take on Christianity in which ants also believe in God, preach the gospel, die, and ascend to heaven.
4. Man and the Ants (2022): Professor Wilson was the one who squatted before this flower all his life, not wanting to know its name, and I was the one who squatted before it all my life, wanting to know its name. The apostle Paul gave me the name of that flower of life: "I have been crucified with Christ; it is no longer I who live, but Christ who lives in me; and the life that I now live in the flesh I live by the faith of the Son of God, who loved me and gave himself for me" (Gal. 2:20).

Chapter 6

1. Coward and Distrust (2022): As soon as Lis Chen had crossed the mountain of Kongo, he met two pilgrims coming in the opposite direction; their names were Coward and Distrust. Coward asked, "How can we continue on this road when we encounter more and more dangers?
2. Pilgrims resting under a tree (2022): Christian dozed off under a tree and fell into a deep sleep, dropping the scroll he was holding.
3. The stork that woke up (2017): I try to stay awake, but my flesh often won't let me. Especially when I find peace of mind in my flesh, I tend to settle for that life. Then there was the stork who woke me up.
4. The Storks of the Great Sea of Mengmang (2015): The stork began to turn its flight path almost 90 degrees to the left. The direction it chose was over the Great Sea of China, where there were no islands in sight for it to land.
5. Clouds, Storks and Airplanes (2016): The only place Sanyang found was the lush grass around the runway, where he wandered around trying to catch grasshoppers. It was then that he heard a single gunshot in the distance. He jumped up in surprise and flew away, but he couldn't get very far; his body was already exhausted.

Chapter 7

1. Compassion and Christianity (2020): "How did you come to leave your home and come this way?"

    "I was so afraid that everything around me would be destroyed. I'm just so thankful that the evangelist told me about the narrow gate and that led me to this path. If it wasn't for him, I probably wouldn't have found this way. After Christian finished sharing his story, he was treated to a delicious dinner and was able to rest in peace for the night.

2. Early Church Christians Martyred at the Stake (2022): Christian was led into a study where he was told that Charity. Piety and Discernment showed Christian the books that recorded the events of a very long time ago. They also showed him the records of the burning of the early Christians.

3. The Mountain of Joy (2020): As Christian looked south, he saw the Mountains of Joy, which were very beautiful and far in the distance.

4. Mrs. Behrend, my friend Heiner, and Professor Schmidt (2021): Mrs. Behrend was a compassionate person who took care of me like a parent so that I could be married in a German church. I met my friend Heiner by chance in the German church; he was also my German teacher. Prof. Schmidt was my advisor, a wise man who gave me a scholarship from the German government so that I could concentrate on my research in peace.

5. The Stork Village (2010): There are quite a few stork villages in Europe outside of Germany. The ones I mostly visited are in Germany and France, especially the stork village in Ribeauville, Alsace, France, which is one of the most beautiful in the world.

6. The Last Supper (2022): The story of the Eucharist in the Bible is the story of Jesus, "who, being in the form of God, did not count equality with God a thing to be grasped, but emptied himself, taking the form of a servant, being made in the likeness of men, and being found in the likeness of men, he humbled himself and became obedient to the point of death, even death on a cross" (Phil 2:6-8).

Chapter 8

1. Apollyon (2022): Leaving his beautiful home, Christian was confronted by a great monster. His name was Aboluon Apollyon (the lion of the abyss, Rev. 9:11), and in fear Christian hesitated whether to turn and run or to face him.
2. Job (2022): Who art thou that thou shouldest question my wisdom with thy ignorant and vain words? Now gird up thy loins, and stand up like a blacksmith, and answer my question. Were you present when I laid the foundation of the earth, and dost thou know who designed it, and dost thou know who laid the measuring line on it?
3. The Early Church (2023): Jesus goes up on a mountain and preaches about how blessed the blessed are. He lists eight blessings: "Blessed are you who feel that you have lost what is most precious to you. Blessed are you who feel that you have lost what is most precious to you, for then you will be embraced by the one who is most precious to you."
4. The Woman and the Stork (2015): Our neighbor Japan had already released its first storks back into the wild, with the crown prince and crown princess attending the reintroduction ceremony. And in the U.S., President Clinton personally announced to the American people the restoration of the endangered American bald eagle. The Lord is telling us to let go of all this.
5. Suspicious Couple (2022): The President appeared before the people with the writing of a prince on his hand. The First Lady appeared to be in a shamanic state, controlling the President at will.

Chapter 9

1. The valley of the shadow of death (2022): When we walk through the valley of the shadow of death, we live in fear, doubt, and anxiety. Though I walk through the valley of the shadow of death, I will fear no evil, for God is with me.
2. The Wanton (2014): She didn't defile herself, of course, but it reminded me of a verse from a book I read a while back: 'Her steps go out into the streets…' (Prov. 5:5). I closed my eyes so I wouldn't be tempted by her dazzling appearance, and she walked away, cursing all the way, and I continued on my way.
3. Prayer (2018): There was nothing more I could do for the storks and their inhabitants except to pray to God daily. I walked and walked and walked, thinking that my pilgrimage must not end as it was, hoping that prayer would carry me through the dreary underbelly of death.
4. Faithful, Christian, and Talkative (2022): At this time a chatterbox was walking along the road. "Friend, where are you going, are you on your way to heaven?" Yes, I am on my way to heaven, and I will gladly accompany you if you wish. "Yes, I am on my way to heaven, and I will gladly accompany you if you wish.
5. The Kiss of Judas Iscariot (2021): After years of teaching, preaching, healing, and doing as He pleased, He was now completely in the hands of His enemies. Judas was an instrument of God's work, but today I confess that Judas is not unimportant to me.

Chapter 10

1. The Merchant and Faithful (2022): A merchant asked, "What on earth are you looking for?" "We seek the truth," replied Faithful.

The merchant, who witnessed this, became suspicious of the men and reported them to the market owner. The two pilgrims were caught by the market owner and tried for disturbing the order of the market.

2. Court of Vanity (2015): One day the state brought me to court in the name of a stork. The crime was unauthorized use of state land. I was accused of building a stork aviary without notifying the state. I went to court because I was accused of using state land without notifying the government.

3. Martyrdom of the Pilgrims (2019): Judge; "Bring one of them to me, make an example of him, and he shall be beheaded immediately. If you are still confused, I will make an example of the other." On a cold, snowy winter day, Faithful was forced to die a horrible death by hanging from a tree on a mountain slope.

4. A girl carrying a baby (2016): My family left the countryside at an early age, and my father and mother worked as traders. I had an older sister who was eight years older than me, and she was the firstborn in our family, so she raised me to the point of carrying me around. The eldest daughter was the breadwinner in those days because both parents had to work in business.

5. The Samaritan Woman (2022): There is a scene in the Bible where a Samaritan woman meets Jesus. Jesus asks this Samaritan woman, who has come out to draw water, for a drink of water. When she asks him, "You are a Jew, how can you ask me, a Samaritan woman, for a drink of water?" he replies, "Because you know that God is generous and I am a Samaritan woman. "If you knew the generosity of God and who I am, you would have asked me for a drink and I would have given you living water.

Chapter 11

1. Obsession, Money Lover, and the Old Man of the City of Greed (2021): Two pilgrims were walking along the road when they met Obsession, Money-Loving, and the Old Man. They were the disciples of Mr. Chuk-jae, who lived in the City of Greed, where he taught them violence, deception, flattery, lies, and all the tricks of the trade in the name of faith.
2. The man who paints pictures in Insadong (2004): In Insadong, Professor Yoon Hoseop, a professor of environmental design at Kookmin University, was already working on environmental protection. There was a time when he tried to inform the citizens that the last storks in Korea had been shot by poachers and had completely disappeared, and that we should introduce and breed storks from Russia to regenerate our polluted nature.
3. Do you know my grandfather (2022): When my daughter's baby is born and becomes a girl, I imagine that she will stand in front of the parliament and ask the question, "Do you know my grandfather?" "He stood in front of parliament every day to make the Stork Law".
4. To receive a little child (2022): Jesus said to welcome a little child because a little child has a heart that does not judge anyone.

Chapter 12

1. Castle of Doubt Dungeon (2022): "Where do you come from, and why have you come to my land?" cried the giant of despair. "We are pilgrims and we have lost our way," replied the Christian. The giant dragged them away and locked them in a dungeon, where they spent days without a sip of water or a crumb of bread.

2. Drunkenness (2022): A terrible thing happened to my daughter, who was born into a beautiful family in Germany. She is a born-again Christian. I thought she was a good and intelligent daughter, but as an adult she often got drunk at dinner parties and lost her mind. She also developed sleepwalking symptoms, wandering the streets alone at night and not being able to find her way home.
3. Peter in prison (2023): A miracle happened to Peter, who was imprisoned for his fervent prayers, when the prison gates were opened (Acts 12:1-10).

Chapter 13

1. The Peak of Error (2022): In the distance, there was the sound of a burning fire, the screams of the tormented, and the smell of sulfur. "This is the road to hell, the road hypocrites usually take.
2. The Seven Devils (2022): On a dark road, I saw a man bound with seven strong ropes being dragged by seven demons. The demons were dragging him to a gate on the side of a hill that pilgrims had seen before (Matt. 12:24; Prov. 5:22).
3. Baby swallows (2018): Throughout my life as an animal behaviorist, I've often wondered if animals love the way humans do. It's not an easy question to answer because I'm a zoologist, so I don't study them from the perspective of love as it is felt by humans. We know from the Bible that God did not entrust the care of creation to animals, but to humans.

Chapter 14

1. Little Faith (2022): Little Faith had a sincere but unfortunately fragile faith. It could be the faith of our neighbors who are not

always vigilant and careful, who are swayed by the ways the world offers, who suffer from Satan's manipulations, and who are prone to fall into his traps.

2. Doubting Thomas (2023): The Bible gives us many examples of the lack of faith of Jesus' disciples. First, there's Thomas the Doubter, who refused to acknowledge Jesus' resurrection until he touched the nail marks. "Do you believe because you have seen? Blessed are those who believe without seeing," says Jesus.

3. O you of little faith!" (2022): After a while, when Peter saw the wind blowing on the sea, he was afraid and fell into the water, crying out, "Lord, save me. Jesus stretched out His hand and caught him and said, "O you of little faith, why did you doubt?"

4. Nicodemus Seeking Jesus Nicodemus (2022): Jesus answered and said to him, "Truly, truly, I say to you, unless a man is born again, he cannot see the kingdom of God. Nicodemus said to him, "How can a man fly when he is old, unless he is born a second time into his mother's womb?" Jesus answered him, "Verily, verily, I say unto thee, Except a man be born of water and the Spirit, he cannot enter into the kingdom of God.

Chapter 15

1. Atheists (2022): On my pilgrimage, I also encounter atheists and ignorance who consistently insist that there is no God. They mock me, saying that the Jesus I believe in is a lie and that God doesn't exist at all.

2. The Devil Sits Ignorance at the Gates of Heaven (2025)

3. The Cross of Jesus and the Two Prisoners (2021): What is important to me now is that the moment we believe that Jesus died on the cross for our sins, we are given new life. It is truly like the prisoner

hanging next to the cross of Jesus, realizing that we can go to paradise with just one moment of confession.
4. People Carrying the Body of Jesus (2022): When I saw the scene where a man named Joseph of Arimathea, who had just died on the cross, was carrying the body of Jesus, I thought, "Jesus has been crucified and this is the end of it.
5. The Risen Jesus and Peter (2022): After his resurrection, Jesus came to the shore of Galilee and ate with his disciple Peter.

Chapter 16

1. The People of the Land of Beulah (2023): The two pilgrims went to a land where birds were singing all the time, the land was covered with flowers, and they could hear the cooing of doves. The sun shone in this land day and night. This was the borderland of heaven, and the pilgrims enjoyed a sweet rest.
2. The Singing Lark (2016): Amidst the flowers of the land of Hala, a magpie sang a song. In a moment, the naturalist's eyes caught the sight of two lorikeets competing for mates. It was an ecstatic moment in the life of a single creature, and it struck him that there was too little terminology to describe it as just a bird's courtship dance. For the Creator, there seems to be no other word than "ecstasy.
3. Jesus Heals the Blind Man (2023): The disciples saw this man who was blind from birth and asked Jesus if it was because of the sins of his parents or his own sins; but Jesus gave them an unexpected answer to the reason for his blindness: it was not a punishment for any particular sin, but a way to reveal the glory of God and to introduce people to Jesus who is the light (John 9:3-5).

4. The Woman with the Hemorrhage (20-22): In the Bible (Mark 5:28-34), a woman with a hemorrhage touches the hem of Jesus' garment and is immediately healed. Jesus says, "Your faith has saved you. This salvation happened once and for all. If there is one thing I hope and pray for, it is to touch the hem of Jesus' garment as I watercolor the characters in the Tenebraeus.
5. Jesus Washing the Disciples' Feet (2022): "Now my body is one step closer to the river of death!" and the realization that I have to give up all my life so far. But only through union with the Body of Christ do I know the full meaning of my body. My body is so much more than an expendable instrument of pleasure and pain.

Chapter 17

1. Two Pilgrims Crossing the River of Death (2022): "For you, the height and depth of the hill to heaven are of no consequence, for you have already cast your flesh into the river." When Christian and Hope heard these words, their hearts fluttered. They really didn't feel the weight of the flesh.
2. Farewell to Purmi the stork (2016): Facing the river of death, can I face death like Purmi? It seems clear that nowadays how we face death is more important than how we are born. The words of the Bible's Psalm (73:4-5), "They have no pain in death, and their strength is strong; they have no sorrow like others, and no calamity like others," become my fervent prayer.
3. Jesus on the donkey (2022): I am on a pilgrimage, and now the Lord says to me, "You see a colt tied up that no one has ridden yet; untie him and bring him to me. And if anyone asks you how to untie it, say, 'The Lord will use it'" (Luke 19:30-31); I want to obey the words, 'The Lord will use it.

4. The Risen Jesus (2022): After the crucifixion, He rose on the third day as prophesied in the Bible. For 40 days, He did not appear to Annas, Caiaphas, Herod, or Pilate, who had condemned Him to death; nor to Nicodemus, His humble disciple; nor to Joseph of Arimathea, who buried Him.
5. Jesus talking to two people on the road to Emmaus (2022): Two men in despair, and the Lord looks into their hearts. Jesus already knew from experience what our human despair is; he knew death and the grave, and he knew our finitude.
6. Globa and his friend (2023): The moment Globa and his friend recognized Jesus in the breaking of the bread, they no longer needed His physical presence as a condition for their new hope. Their relationship with Jesus became so intimate that His strangeness was wiped away. They no longer needed His physical manifestation as a basis for hope because He was so close.

ABOUT THE AUTHOR

Dr. Si-Ryong Park (PhD): Dr. Park is a professor emeritus at Korea University, a member of the Saemun An Church, and currently serves as the supervising professor for KBS's Animal Kingdom. He has served as a consultant for nature documentaries on KBS and MBC, and as the chief professor of the Class 1 endangered species stork restoration project. As a natural scientist, he has written many books, including "Where Storks Can't Live, People Can't Live" (Carpenter's Bookstore), "The Story of an Unfinished Life" (Three Bears), "Storks - Flying in Nature" (Jisungsa), "Landscapes with Storks" (Jisungsa), "Drunken Elephants Are Increasing" (Woongjin Publishing House), and "Animal Behavior Stories" (Consonants and Vowels).

Self-Portrait (2023)

* The watercolors in this book were painted mainly with watercolor paints on a 48.5x37cm sheet of Korean paper, with some ink and acrylic paints.

ENDORSEMENTS

"*The Pilgrim's Progress* is a Christian classic. A classic is a book that speaks to all people in all times, but can be read anew depending on the reader's lens and perspective. This book is a biologist, Prof. Shi-Ryong Park, who reads The Book of the Pilgrim's Progress as a creed. Prof. Park painted watercolors as he followed the Pilgrim's Progress. This biologist turned painter has published a Pilgrim's Confession. While re-reading and painting *The Pilgrim's Progress*, he confesses that he has shaken off the shadow of death and gained the assurance of salvation. Prof. Park's beloved book, Following the Stork, is the same old story, but the confession is still new. I recommend this book with the hope that we too will follow the stork on this pilgrimage, meet Prof. Park's beloved stork, meet the Lord anew, and meet together in the distant city of Zion."

Rev. Dong-won Lee, a fellow the pilgrim
(Senior Pastor of Global Mission Church)

John Bunyan's book, *The Pilgrim's Progress*, is an essential work for Christians and is one of the most widely read Christian books in the world. Although there are several commentaries, it is quite difficult to actually read. Park's *The People of Pilgrim's Progress* contains in-depth meditations, explanations and personal stories of faith, illustrated with watercolours. This book is a guide to interpreting *The Pilgrim's Progress* from a scientist's point of view, enriching it with a variety of perspectives. It will give you the opportunity to rediscover a great classic.

Sang Hak Lee, Senior Pastor of Saemooan Church

www.ingramcontent.com/pod-product-compliance
Lightning Source LLC
Chambersburg PA
CBHW040250170426
43191CB00018B/2368